Franklin Institute Philadelphia, Pa.

Commemorative Exercises at the fiftieth Anniversary of the Franklin Institute

Of the State of Pennsylvania for the Promotion of the Mechanic Arts

Franklin Institute Philadelphia, Pa.

Commemorative Exercises at the fiftieth Anniversary of the Franklin Institute
Of the State of Pennsylvania for the Promotion of the Mechanic Arts

ISBN/EAN: 9783337192501

Printed in Europe, USA, Canada, Australia, Japan

Cover: Foto ©ninafisch / pixelio.de

More available books at **www.hansebooks.com**

COMMEMORATIVE EXERCISES

AT THE

FIFTIETH ANNIVERSARY

OF THE

FRANKLIN INSTITUTE

OF THE STATE OF PENNSYLVANIA FOR THE PROMOTION OF THE MECHANIC ARTS.

HELD ON FRIDAY EVENING, FEBRUARY 6, 1874,

AT THE

MUSICAL FUND HALL.

PHILADELPHIA:

HALL OF THE INSTITUTE,

SEVENTH STREET BELOW MARKET STREET.

1874.

INTRODUCTION.

At the stated meeting of the Franklin Institute, held in December, 1873, the president called attention to the fact that an entry in the first minute book showed that during the latter part of the year 1823 preliminary meetings were held in the city of Philadelphia, which led to the foundation of the Institute during the early part of 1824. He stated that the propriety of some formal recognition by the Society of the completion of its first fifty years had been discussed among some of its older members. Upon motion of Mr. Hector Orr, a resolution was passed, appointing a committee to consist of five members, including the president of the Institute, as chairman, to devise and carry out an appropriate celebration of the Anniversary. The committee consisted of Messrs. Coleman Sellers, Hector Orr, Frederick Fraley, Bloomfield H. Moore, and William P. Tatham.

The meeting which had been held on February 5, 1824, having been decided on as the one which most surely marked the permanent foundation of the Institute as a society, it was deemed advisable, if possible, to hold the commemorative meeting on that day; but inasmuch as no suitable hall could be obtained for the evening of the 5th of February, the following day, namely, the 6th, was fixed upon; and at the meeting of the Institute in January, it was resolved that "When we adjourn we adjourn to meet at the Musical Fund Hall, on the evening of February 6th."

The meeting was public, and largely attended, in spite of the inclemency of the weather, the evening being marked by one of the heaviest snow-storms of the season.

The Programme for the evening was published as follows:—

FRANKLIN INSTITUTE.

1824–1874.

PROGRAMME OF EXERCISES

AT THE

MUSICAL FUND HALL.

FRIDAY EVENING, FEBRUARY 6, 1874.

MUSIC.

ASSEMBLY CALLED TO ORDER BY
Mr. COLEMAN SELLERS,
President of Franklin Institute.

MUSIC.

ADDRESS BY Hon. FREDERICK FRALEY,
Treasurer of Franklin Institute.

MUSIC.

ADDRESS BY ROBERT E. ROGERS, M.D.,
Professor of Chemistry in University of Pennsylvania, and Vice-President of Franklin Institute.

MUSIC.

ADDRESS BY HENRY MORTON, Ph.D.,
President of Stevens Institute of Technology, Hoboken, N. J., and late Secretary of Franklin Institute.

MUSIC.

CLOSING ADDRESS BY Mr. COLEMAN SELLERS,
President of Franklin Institute.

COMMEMORATIVE·EXERCISES

FIFTIETH ANNIVERSARY OF THE FRANKLIN INSTITUTE OF
THE STATE OF PENNSYLVANIA FOR THE PRO·
MOTION OF THE MECHANIC ARTS.

HELD AT MUSICAL FUND HALL, FEBRUARY 6, 1874.

AT 7½ P. M. the Board of Managers welcomed the
invited guests in the lower room of the hall, and at
8 o'clock precisely, they conducted them to the seats
provided for them on the stage. After prelude of
music by the orchestra, the President, Mr. COLEMAN
SELLERS, called the meeting to order and said:—

LADIES AND GENTLEMEN: The object of this meeting is to commemorate the completion of fifty years
of active usefulness of the Franklin Institute. Half
a century ago some earnest mechanics met together
to found an Institution for the promotion of the
mechanic arts. How well the work then started
prospered you all know. It has been deemed fitting
that the ceremonies of this evening should so far as
is possible tell the story of the Society's history,
and also indicate the progress made in the arts and
sciences during the period of its existence. A society
founded so long ago, must of necessity have lost
from its roll of living members many of its earliest
friends. But few of those who signed their names
to the first pages of that honorable list are now
living. Of those who remain, some have long since

2

withdrawn from active participation in the work of this Institution. Among these was one at whose office some of the preliminary meetings were held. I allude to Mr. George Washington Smith. He was invited to address you this evening, but his failing health prevented, and he now writes:—

FEBRUARY 5th, 1874.

GENTLEMEN: A severe cold, which confines me to my chamber, will deprive me of the great pleasure of attending the Fiftieth Anniversary of the founding of the now venerable Franklin Institute. I regret this the more, as I am now the only survivor of the *original* founders of the Society (some months *before* the meeting, which organized the Society, on the 5th of February, 1824). Some members yet remain of those who joined the Institute at this latter date (at the meeting at the court-house in this city), and also still feel an unabated interest in the welfare of the body which they ushered into existence.

I fervently trust that, now we have entered into years of discretion, we shall in the ensuing half century equal and even surpass the useful labors of the past, and that we will not permit any of our numerous progeny in the United States to carry off the palm which has so long decorated our paternal brow—and that in the next generation the Centennial celebration may have nothing to regret in the comparison with the present.

I remain, Gentlemen of the Committee of the Franklin Institute, with great regard, your friend,

GEO. WASHINGTON SMITH.

To Messrs. SELLERS, TATHAM, FRALEY, MOORE, and ORR.

Among those who early joined the Institute was
a young man intimate with its early founders; he
alone of all, remains yet in active co-operation in the
work of the Society. During the entire period of
its existence since his connection with it, he has held
prominent position in its board of management.
During these years he has taken active part in much
that has tended to benefit his fellow citizens. He
has been selected to relate the history of the Institute, for he has helped to make that history, and
his mature mind has made him a leader in its
councils. To-day he stands in our midst, one of our
most valued citizens, faithful in all his trusts, and prominent in the councils of trade, as he was for years
in the council of the State. Ladies and Gentlemen,
it is with pride I announce him as historian, and
introduce to you the Hon. FREDERICK FRALEY, Treasurer of the Franklin Institute.

ADDRESS OF HON. FREDERICK FRALEY.

MR. PRESIDENT:

I thank you most cordially for your eloquent and
flattering introduction to this meeting. If there
were anything calculated to disturb my equanimity,
it would be found in the compliments you have paid
to me, for my long connection with, and services to
the Franklin Institute. But I shall rely on the
abundance of my materials, for presenting to this
audience in the limited time which your arrangements allow, a brief sketch of the history of our
Institution. I shall avail myself of the privilege
you have so courteously granted me, when prepar-

ing my remarks for publication, so to amplify and
collate them, that they may in some respects be
worthy of this great occasion for our rejoicing. I
esteem it a very great honor to have been selected
as the historian of the Institute; and, if I shall fail
in *words* to do full justice to my subject, I shall not
fail in feeling that I ought to put into my utter-
ances the obligations I personally owe to the Institute for the many benefits I have derived from
my long connection with it.

LADIES AND GENTLEMEN:

Upwards of fifty years ago there were two young
men residing in the city of Philadelphia, wholly
unknown to each other, and in different walks of
life, who conceived the same idea, for founding a
new institution for diffusing a knowledge of science
among mechanics and manufacturers. One of them
was the late SAMUEL V. MERRICK, then not quite
twenty-one years of age, who had been bred in a
merchant's counting-house, and, up to the time of
which we are speaking, considered himself devoted
to commercial pursuits. But one of those casualties
which overturn occasionally business establishments,
had fallen upon a firm engaged in the manufacture
of fire engines, to whom the uncle of Mr. Merrick (the late highly honored and esteemed John
Vaughan) had loaned a considerable amount of
money, and for which he had been obliged to take
the property of the firm. Mr. Vaughan made several
unsuccessful efforts to sell the property so acquired,
and at length, in despair of getting anything out of
it, suddenly said to his nephew, one morning: "Sam,
how would you like to be a mechanic?" The youth-

ful clerk responded, "Uncle, I am willing to do anything you may recommend;" and behold by a speedy
transformation the clerk changed into a machinist!
Mr. Vaughan immediately formed a partnership between his nephew and the late JOHN AGNEW; and
the firm continued for many years in existence, with
very favorable results. But Mr. Merrick, in his new
vocation, soon found that he was not a mechanic,
and needed information and instruction to make
him one.

At that time there existed in Philadelphia an
association of mechanics, which met at short intervals, for the consideration of mechanical and scientific subjects, and for mutual improvement by con-
versation and discussion. Mr. Merrick sought to
become a member of this body, obtained a nomina-
tion, but, to his mortification and chagrin, was *blackballed*. He was in almost daily intercourse with the
gentleman who proposed him for membership; and
the subject of his rejection was freely spoken of.
This friend was the late WILLIAM KNEASS, of Philadelphia, then a copper-plate engraver, an artist of
much repute and merit in those days; and afterwards the engraver and die-sinker in the Mint of
the United States, which honorable and responsible
office he filled for many years. In one of these con-
ferences Mr. Kneass said, jestingly: "Why don't
you get up a new Institution to suit yourself?" Although this was said in jest, our young friend took
it to heart, thought over it, and finally called on
Mr. Kneass, and exacted from him a promise, that
he would attend a meeting for the purpose of con-
sidering such a project.

Mr. Merrick accordingly called such a meeting, to
be held at the hall of the American Philosophical

Society; but no one attended. He renewed his call for another meeting, with the same result; and then, having called on Mr. Kneass to remonstrate with him for his desertion, that gentleman said: "If you are really in earnest about this matter, I will tell you who will help you;" and he then narrated to him the history of an abortive attempt made some time before by Professor WILLIAM H. KEATING, of the University of Pennsylvania, to establish an institution somewhat like that which had been conceived by Mr. Merrick.

Professor William H. Keating was the other of the two young men of whom I have just spoken. He had received a thorough liberal education, had graduated with honor at our University, and then went abroad to perfect his scientific training in the polytechnic and mining schools of France and Switzerland.

He returned full of zeal for the diffusion of science applied to agriculture and the mechanic arts, and the Trustees of the University of Pennsylvania, entering cordially into his views, established a Professorship of Chemistry, in its application to Agriculture and the Mechanic Arts, and elected Mr. Keating, then just arrived at manhood, to fill the honorable and novel position.

On the subjects of his Chair, Professor Keating delivered several courses of lectures, and opened a laboratory for the instruction of students, in the basement of the old University building, at Ninth Street, between Chestnut and Market Streets. The house had been built as a residence for the Presidents of the United States, by the State of Pennsylvania; but, not being needed for that purpose, in consequence of the removal of the seat of government of

the United States to Washington City, it was sold
to the University by the State. It was taken down
in 1829 to give place to the two College Halls which
lately stood on the same site; and now the venerable
institution, in which this start in applied science
was first made in our country, has risen in greater
glory and usefulness, in West Philadelphia.

While working earnestly in the sphere to which
he had been called, Mr. Keating sought to interest
his friends and others in an enlarged scheme for
scientific instruction; and he also had called meetings which proved abortive. He supposed that it
was practicable to get the fund given by the Will of
Christopher Ludwig (late Baker-General to General Washington), for the support of a Charity School,
transferred to an institution of higher aims in instruction. And especially did he hope for this, because, by the public school system then recently
established in Philadelphia, the establishment and
support of purely charitable schools had been superseded. But in this praiseworthy attempt he failed,
and he and Mr. Merrick were both stranded in their
hopes. And now, by the kind intervention of Mr.
Kneass, these two ardent men were brought together. Mr. Kneass gave Mr. Merrick a history of
Mr. Keating's efforts, and advised him to call and
see him. This Mr. Merrick speedily did, and, introducing himself, the kindred spirits went earnestly to
work in concert. They compared notes; looked into
the history and objects of the Andersonian Institution
at Glasgow; and finally agreed to make another
effort to get a meeting, under the shadow of whose
authority they might make an appeal to the public.

Such a meeting was accordingly convened, and

tradition, and some memoranda, indicate that the following gentlemen attended: SAMUEL V. MERRICK, THOMAS FLETCHER, MATTHIAS W. BALDWIN, DAVID H. MASON, and ORAN COLTON.

A committee was appointed, consisting of some of those present, and of others selected outside, who were supposed to be willing to unite; and James Ronaldson, Samuel R. Wood, Samuel V. Merrick, M. T. Wickham, W. H. Keating, Thomas Fletcher, and James Rush were appointed to draught a plan of organization, constitution, etc. etc.

The preparation of these details was confided to Mr. Merrick, and he states that, when he presented them to Mr. Wood, he said: "Thee need not read them; I am perfectly willing to adopt them; but thee cannot succeed in establishing thy Institute." Mr. Wood then described to him certain professional jealousies which he said were prevailing in the city; and if either side joined Mr. Merrick in carrying out his plan, it would be sure to be attacked by the other, and thus inevitably become partisan in its character. The small meeting was again convened, the plan approved, and Messrs. Merrick and Keating, nothing daunted, prepared to carry it into execution.

They called to their aid Dr. Robert E. Griffith, and George Washington Smith, Esq., who happily still survives to share in the glory of this anniversary. And these four young men, taking the Philadelphia Directory in their hands, selected from it the names of some 1200 to 1600 citizens, whom they thought might possibly take an interest in such a work, and invited them, by circular letters, to attend a meeting to be held at the county court-house, at

Sixth and Chestnut Streets, on the evening of the 5th of February, 1824, when and where the long cherished project was to be submitted for final approval.

I must here pause for a moment to make a brief comment on this history of the labors of the real founders of the Institute.

In the year 1866, Mr. Merrick placed in my hands a letter* in which he very amply records his own labors in the good work, and the hearty co-operation he received from Professor Keating. As the time has now come in which I am fully justified in making that letter public, I shall place a copy of it at the disposal of the Institute for publication, as part of the proceedings of the evening.

Professor Keating, so far as I know, never prepared any account of his own labors in the great work, and he has left it to tradition, and the memory of loving friends, to give him his proper share of honor.

My own acquaintance with both of these noble-hearted and generous men dates from about the year 1823, when I attended the lectures of Professor Keating in the University, and when I was associated with Mr. Merrick as a member of the Philadelphia Hose Company, the first hose company that was established in the city, and whose honorable record for many years was the pride and glory of its members.

During the whole of the remainder of their lives, I was the intimate friend of both, and it is a gratification to me of the purest and most exalted character, that I am permitted to stand here, upon this occa-

* See letter at close of this article, p. 39.

sion, and bear my hearty testimony to their worth and virtues.

We have now reached the time when the public meeting was held. The citizens responded most cordially to the call, and the court-house was filled to overflowing.

Mr. JAMES RONALDSON (a Scotchman by birth, but an American in every fibre, who was himself engaged in mechanical pursuits, originally a baker, but then a type founder, doing in that line the most extensive business in the United States) was selected to preside.

PETER A. BROWNE, Esq., then an eloquent and distinguished member of the Philadelphia bar, made an earnest and effective speech, in which he sketched the plan and purposes of the new Institution, and his speech was warmly applauded. He was followed by others in earnest and eloquent remarks; a letter was read from NICHOLAS BIDDLE, Esq., then in the acme of his reputation, giving his approval and tendering membership and support.

The Constitution was submitted, considered, amended, and then unanimously adopted.

Lists were then circulated, on which those present enrolled themselves for membership.

A committee was appointed to nominate candidates for officers and managers, and to take the needed order for holding an election on the 16th of the same month. At this meeting I enrolled myself as a member, although not quite of age, and have continued that membership to this day, and may with truth say to the Institute, that " nought but death shall part thee and me!"

By the time the election was held, the roll contained between 400 and 500 members.

Mr. Ronaldson was elected President, and held the office until the year 1842.

The Board of Managers then chosen, of whom, of course, Merrick and Keating were members, went energetically to work, and soon had the Institute thoroughly organized.

Standing Committees on Instruction; on Inventions; on Premiums and Exhibitions; on the Library; and on Models and Minerals, were appointed, and took hold of their duties with zeal and earnestness.

Professorships of Chemistry; of Natural Philosophy and Mechanics; and of Architecture, were forthwith established, and respectively filled by the election of Professor Keating to the first, Professor Robert M. Patterson to the second, and William Strickland, Esq., to the third.

And here I may be permitted to pause and say a word about the University of Pennsylvania, and its ancient and continued interest in and aid to the Institute. Profs. Keating and Patterson both held chairs in that Institution, when they were called into our service, and from that day to the present time our relations to the University have been cordial and complete, for of her gifted Professors we have had, in addition to those already named, Alex. Dallas Bache, John F. Frazer, Henry Reed, and Roswell Park, and from her Medical Department, Professors Hare, James Rogers, and Robert E. Rogers.

The first course of lectures was delivered in the old Academy building, on Fourth, near Arch Street, belonging to the University of Pennsylvania; the use of the building being granted to us by the trustees.

In addition to the lectures on the subjects above named, there were a number of volunteer lectures, delivered by members of the Institute, on various subjects connected with science and the arts.

The foundations thus laid for instruction were rapidly enlarged, and to those like myself, who have been of them and in them for half a century, their proportions and usefulness have been really wonderful.

Soon a school, in which should be taught architectural and mechanical drawing, was established, and it was rapidly filled with pupils. Among the earliest of these was my friend, who is now sitting on the platform, almost as venerable-looking as myself, THOMAS U. WALTER, Esq., then a young bricklayer, but, thanks to that school, afterwards the accomplished and successful architect of the Girard College, then Professor of Architecture in the Institute, and finally commending himself and his works to posterity as the architect of the Capitol at Washington.

But, not content with this special school, the Managers determined to establish another, in which all the useful branches of English Literature and mathematics, and the ancient and modern languages should be taught: in short, a high school. This was placed under the charge of WALTER R. JOHNSON, Esq., with able assistants, and was soon filled with pupils. The Drawing School has been very successfully continued down to the present day, and is now more flourishing than ever before, but the High School was discontinued after a few years' time upon the resignation of Mr. Johnson. By this time the public schools of the city had been much improved by the introduction of new methods of instruction, and the establishment of the Central High School of Philadelphia supplied all the needs that our High School was intended to provide for. The Department of Instruction, with various changes and enlargement of the features, has continued in successful operation down to the present time. Its Professors of Chemistry have been W. H. Keating, Franklin Bache, John K. Mitchell, and John F. Frazer, men who were remarkable for the extent of their knowledge, and whose names are identified with the scientific reputation of our city. With the same honorable and enduring notice we place here the names of our Professors of Natural Philosophy and Mechanics, Robert M. Patterson, Thomas P. Jones, Walter R. Johnson, and John C. Cresson. My space will not permit me to name all their successors, who, taking up their mantles, have won, and are continuing to win, laurels in the same fields. Nor can I begin to make a list of those who have contributed by valuable lectures to fill up more effectually the measure of useful instruction that we have diffused. But I see one of them now near me, the venerable Dr. Gouverneur Emerson, who fully forty years ago delivered a course on meteorology—the first of that character, probably, in this country, and who since then has kept up his interest and knowledge of that important part of atmospheric science, and has lived to witness, in the establishment of the Signal Service Bureau of the United States, the recognition and utility of the infant science he was then aiding in ushering into life.

The Committee on Inventions soon became a centre from which radiated the most useful and interesting results. The late ISAIAH LUKENS, a distinguished mechanician, was for many years its chairman, and, with the Professors in the Institute, and such associates as Alexander Dallas Bache, Benjamin Reeves, Samuel V. Merrick, Rufus Tyler, Matthias W. Baldwin, John Agnew, George Washington Smith, John Wiegand, and others, gave wise counsel to inventors, put them in the way of knowing what had previously been accomplished, saved them from the loss of money and of reputation, by showing them when their inventions were not new; and when any matter of real novelty or value was presented, endorsing it most heartily with their approval, and giving that potential aid which would almost certainly secure public recognition and reward.

This committee continued its labors as originally constituted for many years, and upon its suggestions committees were raised for investigating the various forms of water-wheels, for giving economical value to water-power.

On this subject, experiments of great number, and on almost every form of water motor then known, were made, and the results tabulated and commented on in such an exhaustive manner that the report continues to this day to be a most valuable text-book on water-power.

Following this, and in the same lead of practical usefulness, a committee was raised to investigate the causes of explosion on steam-boilers, and in this investigation, the Institute succeeded in getting the co-operation of the government of the United States, an appropriation for defraying the cost of the experiments being made by Congress. But no part of the money so appropriated was paid as compensation to the experimenters. These were all volunteers, devoting many months of valuable time to the investigation, and ascertaining most valuable facts, which have since been utilized for the benefit and safety of the public.

Connected with these experiments on explosions caused by steam, came almost naturally an investigation of the strength of materials. For this purpose, the committee devised testing apparatus of various forms, and applied them in the most extensive and crucial way to the metals, and materials of all kinds used in machines, steam-boilers, buildings, and other branches of the useful arts. The reports on explosions, and on the strength of materials, were published also, and are of equal reputation and use as those on water-power.

The Committee on Inventions was subsequently abolished, and in its place was established the " Committee on Science and Arts." This committee was intended to cover not only the ground originally occupied by the Committee on Inventions, but to embrace a wider field, and to interest in its operation a larger number of members. Every one, therefore, who felt an interest in developing the domains of invention or science, was invited to enroll himself as a member, and thereby to pledge himself to devote his time and knowledge to the service of the committee, and through it to the public. This voluntary association still exists ; and its long course of labors and usefulness is attested by its memoirs, and by the vast number of reports made on inventions and other matters submitted to its scrutiny. And this seems a fitting place to introduce the name of one of the most illustrious of our members, Alexander Dallas Bache. He was the great-grandson of the world-renowned Dr. BENJAMIN FRANKLIN; and in many traits of character resembled his great ancestor. After receiving a sufficient preliminary education to fit him for it, he was appointed a Cadet in the Military Academy of the United States at West Point, and graduated there, after his four years' course, with distinguished honor. He was duly appointed a second-lieutenant in the artillery corps, and placed in charge of the construction of some of the forts in the New England States. A vacancy having occurred in the Professorship of Chemistry and Natural Philosophy in the University of Pennsylvania, he was elected to the chair, and removed to Philadelphia. He soon joined the Institute, and became one of its most prominent and useful members. He served on the Committees of Instruction, Inventions, Publications, and Exhibitions. His knowledge was great, and his aptitude for applying it wonderful.

He became, as it were, a centre around which every department of the Institute could revolve, and, like that other great centre, the sun, he had the faculty of controlling, and keeping in harmony and efficient working order, all who came within his influence.

To him, the investigations on water-power, explosions of steam, and strength of materials, owe much of their value. He supervised the reduction of the results of experiments, tabulated them, and mainly prepared the reports.

To his efforts the organization of the Committee on Science was mainly due. He presided over it for many years, and by his skill and wisdom in selecting its sub-committees, rendered it useful and powerful. After a long service with us, and with the University, and after having laid the foundations for instruction in the Girard College for Orphans, and for the Central High School, he left us to accept the appointment of Superintendent of the Coast Survey of the United States. In this new field of labor and usefulness he was the same patient, devoted, and successful worker, and brought that great national work up to a state of accuracy and comprehensiveness that has challenged the admiration of the world. Until death, he was the warm friend and earnest advocate of the Institute. He was my early schoolmate; the affectionate friend and associate of my manhood; and his virtues and worth are among the most precious of my memories.

One of the methods adopted by the Institute for the promotion of the mechanic arts was to reward inventors, manufacturers, and mechanics, by the distribution of medals and premiums. To this end, the Committee on Premiums and Exhibitions was appointed.

It very soon announced that an Exhibition of American Manufactures would be held in the city of Philadelphia, and published a long list of premiums that would then be awarded. A very extensive circulation of this intention was given by letters addressed to those whose interests would be promoted by the Exhibition, and also by advertisements to direct public attention to the undertaking. It was held in the Carpenters' Hall, in Philadelphia, in the autumn of 1824, and was crowned with complete success. It attracted large crowds of people, who hitherto had had no conception of the extent and

3

variety of our home productions, and reacted in many curious and unexpected ways to bring producers and consumers together, and to diffuse a knowledge of our domestic skill and resources. These Exhibitions were continued at short intervals for many years, and grew in public favor and usefulness; but were suspended a few years ago in consequence of an inability to get a hall of sufficient size for a proper display. It would be impossible to estimate the value of these Exhibitions, for it is only those who, from year to year, watched the progress of manufactures in the United States, as their products were brought together in friendly competition on our tables, that can realize the astonishing developments of our industry which have marked the half century now closed. The Institute, having secured, for an Exhibition to be held in the autumn of the present year, by the liberality of the Pennsylvania Railroad Company, a building of ample size, and in a most favorable location, will resume this well-tried part of its system of operations, and in the coming display, lay the groundwork, and stimulate preparation for the great Centennial International Exhibition, which in 1876 is to commemorate the hundredth anniversary of our existence as a nation.

Without a library, the Institute would have been but half armed; and soon, under the auspices of the committee charged with attention to that feature of the Institution, books began to take their places on our shelves, to accumulate, to be used, and gradually to assume the numbers and variety which now characterize our large and valuable collection.

In natural connection with the library comes the *Journal*. At the outset, the pecuniary means of the Institute were too limited to permit it to venture alone on such a publication. But an arrangement was made with THOMAS P. JONES, Esq., then Professor of Natural Philosophy and Mechanics, to edit and publish a periodical devoted to science and the arts, under the title of the *Franklin Journal*. In this form, and with limited aid from our treasury, the publication was continued until 1828, when the Institute assumed the responsibility of continuing it, under the title of *The Journal of the Franklin Institute;* and so it has continued to this time.

Of the great value of the *Journal*, in diffusing information of varied character, on subjects of science and the arts, you, who have had the best opportunities for judging, can make a proper estimate. I will only say that, to have stood the tests of competition, active and extensive as they have been, furnishes pretty strong proof that it has been well and ably managed; and although its balance sheets do not show an absolute profit in money, the results of its exchanges are on your bookshelves, and are of far more worth than mere money.

And now let us stop for a moment to pay a passing tribute to the memory and worth of an old officer of the Institute, to whom the *Journal* was as the apple of his eye.

You all recollect WILLIAM HAMILTON, for nearly half a century our loved and trusted Actuary. He went in and out before us for this long period, the very embodiment of our Franklin Institute. I became a member of the Board of Managers just after his election in the year 1828.

With the exception of a few years I have been Treasurer or Secretary during his whole term, and these offices brought me into almost daily intercourse with Mr. Hamilton. And I may truly say that I have often marvelled at the devotion which characterized him in our service. The interests of the Institute seemed to be the blood that circulated in his arteries and the marrow of his bones.

Rarely affected by illness, he was always at his post; he knew every detail of our working movements; he was ready to produce book, report, account, or model, at any call; he seemed to know every member; he maintained his good temper and courtesy when often sorely tried; and, by his kindheartedness and good management, kept many from straying from our fold. He was scrupulously honest and trustworthy; and all his thoughts and actions were regulated and controlled by a simple religious and conscientious spirit. No one who knew him thoroughly could fail to love and honor him.

He seemed, at his fourscore years, to have scarcely lost the vigor and elasticity of his manhood; and, within a week of his death, he was discharging every duty of his office as carefully and with as much love and interest as ever. He was a loving and faithful servant; and deserves our gratitude and enduring remembrance.

The editors of the *Journal* have been Thomas P. Jones, A. D. Bache, Charles B. Trego, John F. Frazer, Henry Morton, and William H. Wahl; and as this sketch is going through the press, Professor George F. Barker of the University has assumed that duty.

Among the early committees we find that on Models and Minerals, and, thanks to its labors, we have quite a respectable collection of both; and had we space for more, the contributions of willing inventors and friends would no doubt be large. In our collection are to be found some curious, and interesting specimens of ingenuity. One of these is the model of a machine for producing perpetual motion. This is the work of Isaiah Lukens, before mentioned as Chairman of the Committee on Inventions. He was also one of the early Vice-Presidents. Some of the older of my audience will recollect the excitement caused by the announcement that a Mr. Redheffer had discovered the perpetual motion. Mr. Lukens visited the place of the exhibition of Redheffer's machine, and, after a brief examination, discovered the trick. Returning to his workshop he immediately constructed a machine in imitation of Redheffer's, but with the motor concealed in a different way. He then sent for Redheffer, informed him that he had discovered his trick and fraud, told him that the machine before him was also a fraud, and challenged him to point it out, which Redheffer ineffectually tried to do, and gave up in despair.

But the labors and services of the Institute were not bounded by what we have been describing. The lectures of Mr. JAMES P. ESPY, and his essays on meteorology, and the theories adverse thereto of Redfield and others, caused a large share of public attention to be directed to that subject. Dr. Emerson had awakened our members many years before to its importance; and the Legislature of Pennsylvania made a liberal appropriation for the purchase of instruments, and for the collection of facts by observers in all parts of the State.

The purchase of instruments, the organization of

the corps of observers, and the tabulation and publication of the results, and the whole expenditure of the appropriation, were placed in charge of the Institute. The fund was carefully managed, and for a number of years monthly tables of the observations were published in the *Journal.* Subsequently, the Institute was requested by the State Legislature to examine and report upon our system of weights and measures. A special committee was called, which thoroughly went through the work, and, upon its report, the law was enacted which is now in force for the commonwealth.

The general interest created by the existence and working of the Institute caused more attention to be paid to technology and to science generally; and gave rise to a movement for the establishment of a school of arts in the year 1837. The Institute headed this movement, and applied to the councils of the city for a grant of a large plot of ground in West Philadelphia as a site for the buildings of the proposed school.

This was promptly and cheerfully granted, and the Legislature was appealed to by memorials from all parts of the State, to endow the school by a liberal appropriation. The House of Representatives passed the bill for this purpose, but immediately reconsidered its action, the members seeming to be alarmed at their own courage in venturing so far out of the old paths.

It was well understood, then, that if the bill had reached the Senate it would have been promptly passed; and Governor Ritner had promised to give it his approval. The seed then planted was watched with care, and efforts were often made to resuscitate the enterprise. It was finally taken up by the trustees of the University, among whom are to be found now a number of the active members of the Institute; and, by the cordial concurrence and aid of Dr. Charles J. Stillé, the Provost, the Department of Science was established in the University on a most comprehensive basis, and is now in successful operation. Thus it has been that the philanthropic efforts of Merrick and Keating to start our Institute were crowned with such complete success.

As I have before stated, the first course of lectures was delivered in the old Academy Building on Fourth Street. The Institute very soon rented the lower story of the Old Carpenter's Hall, in the rear of Chestnut Street, east of Fourth Street, a place rendered memorable and almost sacred by the sessions of the first Continental Congress.

By this time we felt so sure of our hold on the public, that we determined to build a hall, and, to carry out this intention, a purchase was made of the lot on Seventh Street between Market and Chestnut Streets.

The corner-stone was laid with appropriate Masonic and other ceremonies, on the eighth day of June, 1825, at noon, and the edifice was erected by contract, from plans and estimates furnished by John Haviland, Esq., the architect. We were obliged to have an eye to revenue from the building, and to aid us in that, then important matter, an agreement was made with the United States, that we would arrange and finish the second story so that it might be occupied as a court-room, and offices for the Circuit and District Courts. When the building was completed, a lease was accordingly made for a term of years at

$1500 per annum. But after a short occupancy, this lease was cancelled, as it was found to be inconvenient for members of the bar to be *so far* from the county court-house at Sixth and Chestnut Streets. The United States then agreed to give up the premises, and to pay $900 per annum for the remainder of the term, and the city rented them the second story of Independence Hall.

The building was completed, and we entered into the occupancy of all except the second story in 1826, and then began to feel that we had got out of our "long clothes."

On the cancellation of the lease to the United States, we obtained possession of the whole building; and therein, all the manifold labors of the Institute have been conceived and carried into execution.

This dear old hall is associated with so many pleasant and useful memories, that whenever removal to a new building has been agitated, it has given rise to strong emotions.

But it has so happened that the intention of removal has several times been seriously considered. It very nearly culminated in the year 1836, when the Masonic Hall property on Chestnut Street west of Seventh Street was purchased by the Institute for the sum of $110,500.

Plans for a new and enlarged hall were prepared by William Strickland, Esq., architect, aided by a committee of the Institute. A plan for a building loan was adopted, and a part of it subscribed for, which enabled the Institute to pay the first instalment of the purchase-money. But the great financial crash of May, 1837, struck our project down, and after vainly struggling for several years to carry it out, we had at last to surrender it, and at a fearful loss of many thousands of dollars. At different times since, projects of removal have been started, but grown wise by the experience of 1837, we have not been again tempted into any uncertain contracts. The old hall has been modified and improved in its interior; and, although small and inconvenient in some respects for our present wants, will not hastily be abandoned.

Mr. James Ronaldson served as President until January, 1842, when he resigned; but he maintained his interest in the Institution until he died, and gave it by his will a legacy of five hundred dollars.

He was succeeded by Samuel V. Merrick, the acknowledged Founder of the Institute, and the man above all others who impressed on it at the beginning, nearly all of its practical features, as Keating did those for its science.

Mr. Merrick held the office of President until January, 1855, when he resigned.

But his resignation of office did not sever him from active duty. As in the beginning, so throughout his whole life, every faculty he enjoyed, every hour that was needful for its service, time, talents, and money, were always ready for the Institute. And if asked to point out his monument, standing in our hall, we should reply " *Circumspice*."

Mr. Merrick was succeeded in the Presidency by John C. Cresson. My relations to Mr. Cresson make it difficult for me to speak of his merits and services. He was elected a member in 1834. He had early in life chosen agriculture for a profession, and, in preparing for it, after receiving a good classical education, he paid considerable attention to the study of chemistry, natural philosophy, and mechanics. He attended the lectures of Professor Keating in the University in 1823. Very soon after his election as a member, he relinquished his agricultural pursuits, and engaged in commercial business in the city. He became an active and useful member of our important committees.

Shortly after the Philadelphia gas-works were built, under the charge of Mr. Merrick, as engineer; Mr. Cresson was appointed superintendent of the works, and subsequently engineer. He gave such evidence of his thorough knowledge of natural philosophy and mechanics that he was elected Professor in 1837, and held that office for several years.

On the resignation of Professor Bache as Chairman of the Committee on Science and the Arts, Professor Cresson was elected its chairman, and still holds that place. As the worthy coadjutor, friend, and associate of Merrick, Keating, Bache, and the other active members of the Institute, he was considered the fittest man to succeed Mr. Merrick. His able administration was universally recognized, and he occupies a high and honorable place in our records and history.

He declined a re-election in 1864, and WILLIAM SELLERS, Esq., was chosen his successor.

Under the administration of this estimable and distinguished mechanical engineer a new impulse was given to the career of the Institute. The plan of organization was modified, and a large sum was raised by Mr. Sellers and his friends to reduce the debt, to repair and alter the hall, and to bring the Institution into more effectual contact with manu-

facturers and mechanics. Professor HENRY MORTON,
who was winning an enviable reputation as a physi-
cist and lecturer, was chosen Secretary ; and with a
liberal salary and enlarged powers was made its chief
executive officer. He was also entrusted with the
editorship of the *Journal*, and, until his election as
President of the "Stevens Institute," devoted his
rare abilities to our service. It is with great pleasure
that I see him here on this occasion, to unite with us
in proclaiming the advantages of such institutions.

One of the principal changes made by the advice
of Mr. Sellers and his friends was to have the whole
of our property represented by stock, the shares of
which could be purchased at a moderate price, and
giving the privileges of membership transferable for
the benefit of heirs or purchasers. The introduction
of these new elements of strength was hailed with
much pleasure by those who had held offices for so
many years. Death had diminished the number of
the old associates, and age and physical infirmity
were depriving them of their ancient ardor and zeal.
But they were still ready, with their old attach-
ment, to aid with their counsel and presence these
new and active workers; and the Institute was
strengthened and benefited by the combination of
such elements.

Mr. Sellers declined a re-election in 1868, and was
succeeded by JOHN VAUGHAN MERRICK, Esq., the
eldest son of the distinguished Founder. He in-
herited all the interest so long held by his father,
and energetically carried out the new and enlarged
policy.

He declined a re-election in January, 1870, and
was succeeded by COLEMAN SELLERS, Esq., who now

holds the office, and is ably and faithfully discharging its duties.

He is also by profession a mechanical engineer, and has won, by his ingenuity and skill, an honorable name in his profession.

In making up this record of our Presidents, it is a remarkable fact that they have all been characterized by the possession of rare gifts of administration and of public confidence.

JOHN SCOTT, a chemist of Edinburgh, gave by his will to the corporation of the city of Philadelphia a legacy for the establishment of a premium, to be given by a medal and money to the inventors of anything new or useful. In the year 1834, the city councils placed the awarding of the Scott's Legacy Medal and Premium in the hands of the Institute, and it has so faithfully and carefully discharged that duty that its stewardship still continues.

In the year 1848, the late ELLIOTT CRESSON, Esq., placed in the charge of trustees a sufficient sum of money to provide a gold medal, which was to be awarded by the Institute to the inventor of any new or useful discovery. As this premium is to be given only for matters of real novelty and merit, it is, of course, rarely issued. The first recipient of it was Gen. Benjamin C. Tilghman, Esq., of Philadelphia, the discoverer of the application of the sand blast, for a variety of useful and ornamental purposes.

And in 1859, URIAH A. BOYDEN, of Boston, Mass., placed in charge of the Institute the sum of one thousand dollars, to be awarded to " any resident of North America who shall determine by experiment whether all rays of light, and other physical rays, are or are not transmitted with the same velocity." The claim to be made in the form of an essay, announcing the result and its manner of ascertainment, to be presented before the first day of January, 1873. The awarding of this premium was placed in the hands of a committee.

Several essays were received, but no one of them was considered of sufficient merit to entitle it to the prize.

Mr. Boyden has generously allowed the premium to remain with the Institute, in the hope that it may be earned by some worthy mathematician.

Having now brought this historical sketch down to the present time, we may be permitted to linger a little while over our personal experiences, and to bear our testimony to the many advantages we have enjoyed from our connection with the Institute. Speaking for myself, I may say, most truly, that it has been to me my school of schools. As an original member, and then a very young man, I was immediately associated with the founders, and with those older and accomplished men who had joined with them. Together we walked for over forty years, not in the wilderness but by pleasant paths, studying by the way all that was new and useful in science and the arts, and accumulating priceless treasures of knowledge.

My friend, Professor Robert E. Rogers, is about to follow me with the wonderful record of the progress of science in the last half century. Modern physical science has been made within that time, and, as each brilliant discovery was announced in chemistry, physics, or mechanics, it was brought into our field in the hall of the Institute, and the

band of brothers there assembled lovingly together
made themselves, in their respective walks, masters
of the new discoveries; and in not a few instances
enlarged and perfected their applications. I am
thankful that for the half century I have been an
active member of the Institute, I owe to its teachings and their influence on my mind very much of
the knowledge and information that have given any
useful influence to my life ; and my earnest prayer
for the young members of it is, that they shall de-
rive as much advantage from its teachings as I have
realized. I see around me here to-night some of the
original members, and others who were speedily
enrolled.

As I entered this hall, I was greeted by one of
the original members, Mr. GEORGE S. LANG, with
vivid reminders of our first meeting at the county
court-house in February 1824. Here also I see on
this platform the venerable forms of my friends,
Henry C. Carey, David S. Brown, Gouverneur Emerson, Thomas U. Walter, and Hector Orr, early and
earnest laborers in the fields I have been describing.

The numbers of the Old Guard are gradually
diminishing, but the golden cord that has bound us
together so long still encircles the survivors. Of the
illustrious dead, how shall I venture to make up the
record ? Merrick, Keating, Patterson, Strickland,
Bache, Peale, Frazer, Lukens, Baldwin, Tyler, were
chiefs on the roll of the departed.

George Washington Smith, Carey, Emerson, Cresson, Wiegand, Booth, Roberts, Trego, still survive,
with their love for the Institute undiminished by age.
Did space permit, I might swell to a large extent
this list of devoted men; but I content myself with
the types I have selected, and say in all sincerity, of

those not named, that the working force of the Institute was imbued with the spirit of such chiefs. I now close my attempt to place before you a history of the Institute.

It has honorably lived for half a century; it is again endowed with the invigoration of youth and earnestness; it has all the experience of the past in its treasure house; it has all the bright promise of the future for its encouragement.

As we now rejoice over what we have accomplished, so may those who come after us celebrate with even more fervor its Centennial. And, when the hundred years are ended, may new hands keep our banner up, waving, in glorious pride, over new victories won for the benefit and improvement of mankind, and cheer the old Institute onward, with the well-earned cry of *Esto Perpetua!*

LETTER OF MR. MERRICK TO MR. FRALEY.

Philad., 11 Sept. 1866.

Dear Fraley—

Reflecting upon our little talk on old times this morning, I have concluded that justice to myself and other friends connected with the early history of the Franklin Institute, calls for such information as you seem to need in relation to its origin. In this I may subject myself to a charge of egotism; but I think you know me well enough to acquit me of any intentional wrong to any one.

I look back on the incipiency of that Institution, feeling that if I had done nothing else in my life, I should have something to be proud of in the part I took in its founding.

You know that I was reared in a counting-house, and destined to a mercantile life.

Circumstances which need not be detailed changed its objects; and at an age before maturity I found myself an owner of a workshop, without a mechanical education and with scarcely a mechanical idea.

On contemplating the position thus assumed I was made aware of two facts: that without knowledge I could not succeed, while it was too late again to go to school; and, secondly, that as a mechanic I was socially degraded, for in those days, as people despised mere mechanics, my own position shared that of my class.

There existed at that time a society of mechanics who statedly met for discussion and mutual improvement, into which I desired admission for the same object. Being proposed, I was blackballed under the influence of personal ill-will entertained by a prominent member.

Well acquainted with Mr. Wm. H. Kneass, engraver, who occupied a shop in Fourth St., in my daily work I frequently called for friendly chat. Mr. K. had proposed me to the Association, and was much annoyed at the issue of the vote.

Discussing the matter with him one day with no very pleasant feelings, he jestingly asked me why I did not start a new society having a wider field of usefulness.

I was very young and had but a limited acquaintance; yet after a night's reflection I determined to act on his suggestion, though I knew he was not serious.

With this view I called a meeting at the Philosophical Hall of some fifteen or twenty gentlemen who I supposed would take an interest in so useful a movement. The night of meeting came, and no one responded to the call.

After talking the matter over the next day with several who professed an interest in the project, I called a second meeting, with a similar result.

A further conference with Mr. Kneass was the consequence of the second failure; to whom I complained that he had not kept his appointment. He then said seriously that he thought I was wasting my time. That it was impossible to unite the mechanics of Philadelphia in such an enterprise, and I had better abandon the idea. I replied that I had a better opinion of the public spirit of Philadelphia, and that I was determined to succeed.

He replied that as I was bent on going forward, he would tell me where I was likely to get help. He then gave me an account of the above abortive movement in the same direction which had been made the year before; and stated that William H. Keating, a young professor, had been secretary of those meetings, and had showed much interest in the success of the plan; and that I would find Mr. Keating at the University in Ninth Street.

I called on Mr. Keating, introduced myself, stated the object of my visit, and asked of him the history of the last failure, and if he would join me in the present movement. Mr. Keating cordially responded and entered heartily into my views.

He gave all the information required as to the former attempt and failure ; and an account of the Andersonian Institute of Glasgow, on which it was proposed to model, in some respects, the new Institution.

After perusing these documents, we had several interviews, during which we agreed upon a name, and sketched a programme of the purposes we proposed to incorporate in the new Institution.

It was then agreed, as a *point-d'-appui* was necessary, to call a small meeting which would by proper action give an official start to the machine. Accordingly I summoned a third meeting, to which four gentlemen responded. Its action was confined to the passage of a resolution approving the design, and to the appointment of a committee to carry out the idea by public meeting or otherwise.

The minute of this meeting is the managers' book, and it consisted of five persons. The correctness of names is somewhat in doubt, as none were taken down at the time, but those which appear were appended some years afterwards from a memorandum in the hands of the chairman. This is, however, of no consequence, as they did not project or found the Institute, but merely passed formal resolutions on which the founders acted.

Having thus obtained the official authority of a meeting, the committee was convened. Mr. S. R. Wood and myself were appointed a sub-committee to draft a constitution. This labor fell to my share, and when ready Mr. Wood was called to revise and adopt it, ready for the general committee.

When commencing to read the draft Mr. Wood stopped me and said, " Thee need not read that paper. I have no doubt it is all right, and I will agree to report it ; but I want to satisfy thee that this Institution can never succeed and had better be abandoned."

I then listened to a long explanation of the quarrel between two rival architects, and learned that there existed such a feud between them and their respective friends that in his opinion they could never coalesce ; and if either party took up the proposed plan, the Institute would be partisan in its character, and be opposed by the other.

I name this to show the obstacles thrown in the way of the

4

incipient Institution, and I think that was the real reason for the failure the year before.

Unconvinced by Mr. Wood's reasoning, the draft of the constitution was reported and adopted by the committee at large, which also agreed upon its presentation for final adoption to a public meeting to be convened for the purpose of forming an association.

Determined that the Institute should not be smothered by rival interests, Mr. Keating and myself, aided by Dr. R. E. Griffith and G. W. Smith, who were deeply interested in its success, had circulars printed to the number of 12 or 1500. One of us read from the Directory probable names, and the others addressed the notes to every person who from his occupation would be likely to favor the movement. These notes were distributed through the post-office, and the result was the assembling of more citizens than could be crowded into the county court-house, the place agreed on.

This meeting, of which no record exists within my knowledge, was presided over by James Ronaldson, Esq., and after the purposes of the proposed Institution had been fully explained by Col. P. A. Browne and others, an animated discussion took place until the subject was fully understood by a highly intelligent assembly, who unanimously accorded their approbation of the purpose in view. After which the constitution was presented, critically discussed, and after amendment was unanimously adopted, and a day fixed for the election of officers from those who should previously enroll their names, and which numbered some three to four hundred.

The election having taken place, the Franklin Institute assumed its position among the Institutions of the State, and has since attained a gratifying pre-eminence.

The meeting was a perfect success; and the novel mode of throwing the Association open to the world without the intervention of cliques, made it universally popular.

I have been, perhaps, more minute in details than would be proper for a public purpose, but having prepared them for your eye, it may be pardoned.

I simply desire to secure a record of these proceedings somewhere, and therefore request that, when you have perused this, you will consign it to one of your "pigeon holes" for future reference, if occasion should occur.

Yours truly,

S. V. MERRICK.

AFTER the music had ceased, which followed Mr. Fraley's address, the President announced the next speaker, saying that, in seeking for some one to speak on the progress of the arts and sciences during the period comprised in the existence of the Franklin Institute, it was but natural that the committee should look to the University of Pennsylvania for a fitting person. The teachers of that great school have been prominent in our scientific work, so that somehow the two institutions seem almost as if connected. Thus, the Professor of Chemistry in the medical department of the University is also a vice-president of the Franklin Institute; being himself not only a chemist and physician, but has shown himself to be a mechanic too in the highest sense of the word; he has made himself familiar with the progress of the mechanic arts, and knows well the part played by the sciences in that progress. I now introduce to the audience Dr. ROBERT E. ROGERS, Vice-President of the Franklin Institute.

ADDRESS OF PROF. ROBERT E. ROGERS.

MR. PRESIDENT—LADIES AND GENTLEMEN:

For a country which will two years hence celebrate *only* its first ONE HUNDREDTH ANNIVERSARY as a Nation, occasions like the present are rare and of peculiar interest.

Fifty years ago, the Franklin Institute of Philadelphia pledged itself to the sciences and the arts; on that occasion it promised them its love and devotion; during the interval that has since elapsed they have lived together in happy companionship. To-night we celebrate their GOLDEN WEDDING.

Permit me, Mr. President, to thank you cordially for the words of compliment with which you have introduced me, and to express my high sense of the honor which the Institute has bestowed in assigning to me the responsible and difficult duty which I am called upon this evening to perform.

This honor I should have felt myself constrained to decline, in view of the almost unlimited range of the theme and an oppressive consciousness of insufficient time—amid my other labors—for the preparation of anything worthy of the occasion, but for the assurance of friends, that all allowance will be made for any short-comings. I have, therefore, consented to attempt to sketch, in brief outline, some of the more important discoveries in science, and improvements in the arts, which have been made during these past fifty years—within the lifetime of the Franklin Institute.

A little more than a hundred years ago, the genius of Watt produced a marvel in the shape of a practical steam engine ;(1)* and Fulton, and Stevens, and others in this country had, a little later, made successful application of it on rivers and lakes. But it was left for the period we are here met to commemorate to spread the network of the iron rail, almost over the surface of the globe; and to introduce the Locomotive—not, it is true, in its perfect form, but in those two *vital* features which, in 1829, were successfully applied by Robert Stephenson— namely, the injection of the exhaust steam into the

* All the references in the text refer to the notes in the Appendix.

smoke-stack, and the multitubular form of boiler; the former originating in the fertile brain of Stephenson, the latter, it is stated, the suggestion of Mr. Booth, who was then in the interest of the Liverpool and Manchester Railway Company; inventions which alone give to the machine that *steam-generating* power adequate to fulfil the requirements of trade and travel, and which, to this day, have not been superseded.(2)*

Who has not read, with enthusiastic admiration, of the competitive trial on the Liverpool and Manchester Railway, of the *Rocket*, the *Novelty*, and the *Sans Pareil*, of October, 1829, in which the former, that of Stephenson, so triumphantly took the prize?

At this period it had been ascertained that, on level tracts and with moderate loads, the tires of the driving wheels might be smooth.

The next result to be accomplished was to dispense with cog-wheels and notched rails, stationary engines and inclined planes, and to enable the locomotive not only to draw at high speed its ponderous train of cars over the level track, but also to climb steep grades by a *power within* itself. This was effected by the discovery made quite within the period we note, that by *sufficiently loading* the engine over the driving wheels, and by increasing the number of the driving wheels, their adhesion is rendered adequate to overcome the increased resistance due to gravity, and to enable it thereby with almost equal facility to cross the mountain as to traverse the plain.(3)

Much credit is due to Mr. Moncure Robinson for

* This is the usually accepted history of these improvements. For another statement see note 2 of Appendix.

his zeal and perseverance in urging the introduction into the service of the Reading Railroad of this class of locomotives, now so almost universally in use.

The interest awakened at home and abroad by the performance of the Gowan & Marx, is so distinctly pointed out by the able writer, M. Michel Chevalier, in his treatise " Histoire et Description des Voies de Communication aux Etats Unis,"(4) and by the late Joseph Harrison, Jr., in his volume the "Locomotive," that I deem it in place to make the quotations given in the Appendix.(5)

To this period belongs also the mighty Marine Engine, and the improved form of propeller,(6) which, revolutionizing navigation, have rendered the ocean also a crowded highway of swiftly moving commerce. Not a few of those here assembled will fail to recall the curiosity and amazement with which they beheld anchored in American waters, in succession, the "Sirius" and the "Great Western," the first steam-ships that had crossed the Atlantic, so proudly solving the great problem that had agitated the nautical and commercial world.(7)

Glancing over the industrial arts, there would seem to be no end to the varied and multifarious directions in which the potent energies of steam have, in these recent years, been applied.

At an earlier period had been invented the cotton gin of Whitney, to take the place of the tedious process of hand picking; and the spinning mule of Cartwright, twisting from the thinnest fibre to the stoutest cable; and the power loom of Arkwright, weaving from the finest gossamer to the coarsest canvas or carpet; but favorably comparing with these inventions, both in ingenuity and value to the world, are the steam printing presses of Hoe, and of Bullock of our own time and country, and of Walter, of England,(8) which, with their almost living fingers, and, as by human guidance, lift, and carry, and turn over for the type the paper to be printed, and are able to throw off an edition of one hundred thousand double-printed sheets within the brief space of a few hours; and the Steam Hammer, in its improved forms, with its delicate touch or giant power that can shape the needle or forge the anchor.

While we have snatched the oar from the sluggish barge, and torn the white canvas from the kissing breeze, and through the agencies of steam have covered the rivers and the seas with those quick and sure messengers of trade, whose wings no current can arrest, and scarcely tide or tempest can delay, so in the manufactory, where the weary horse or fluctuating wind or stream slowly and unsteadily performed their appointed tasks, we have planted the *engine with its highly improved capabilities*, whose untiring energy whirls the spindle or throws the shuttle, and performs besides in its hundred handed dexterity, with new forms of machinery, every variety of labor, from that of pumping, sawing, planing, hoisting, grinding, pounding, boring, threshing, rolling, and propelling the furnace-blast, to that of dragging the ponderous gang plough over the stretches of our western prairies.

It was as far back as 1790 that Galvani evoked the first fact in dynamic electricity; this led to Volta's discovery in 1800 of the Voltaic pile, and the device of the crown of cups; and was followed later in the same year by the startling discoveries by Davy of the true nature of the battery's action, and by its agency of the metals of the alkalies and alkaline earths.

While all honor and admiration are due to each of these gifted philosophers, it was reserved for a period almost within the last half century to witness the experiments of Oersted and Ampère in the deflection of the magnetic needle by the galvanic current, the magnetization of iron by the same influence, by Arago, and within this period, of Sturgeon and our own Prof. Henry(9) to produce the electro-magnet, and of Faraday—the once humble bookbinder—to write his name in letters of gold among men, for his extensive and profound researches in electricity, *static* and *dynamic.*

Upon the combined discoveries and researches of these philosophers is based that second marvel of modern civilization—the Electric Telegraph—the most prominent forms of which are those of Morse and Wheatstone, the Mechanical(10) and the Needle or oscillating, the one for the *land*, the other for the *sea.*

Wonderful as is this achievement, it is but one of the innumerable fruits of these discoveries, which so much contribute to the comfort, enjoyment, and refinement of mankind.

Mark for instance the whole range of Electrochemistry; the decomposition by the galvanic current, of the metallic salts in the processes of electroplating of copper, nickel, silver, and gold, whereby engravings of maps and verniers, busts, medals, and other objects of use and ornament may be reproduced as perfect fac-similes, and the beautiful semblance of the precious metals made to take the place of base and less attractive alloys; and the dissipation of the threatening tumor and treatment of other maladies by its destructive chemical or heating powers.

And then the electro-carbon light whose splendor is only surpassed by that of the sun himself. And again the no less powerful but more convenient ·magneto-electric light, which now glows from the towers of Le Hevre and Dungeness to warn the storm-beaten and bewildered mariner as he approaches the rock-bound coast.(11)

Witness through electro-magnetism the various signal instruments, as the burglar-alarm, the fire-alarm, the factory and depot-watchman's check clock, and more valuable perhaps than many of these, the *chronograph*, by which the longitudes of places on the earth's surface are ascertained with more precision than ever before attained, replacing the old methods of determining the occurrence of celestial phenomena, such as the transit of stars and planets, wherein the observation is recorded directly by the touch of an electro-magnetic trigger, a method known and recognized as the *American method*, instead of by the eye and hand.

In this connection must be named the whole cata-logue of the constant galvanic batteries, those of Daniel, Grove, Bunsen, and Callan, and the water batteries of Gassiot, and that of the Bichromate of Potassium and Sulphuric Ácid, and later, the Gravity battery, without whose agency the manifold modern applications of this subtile power could not have been accomplished.(12) And here too we must mention the steam electrical machine devised by Armstrong, and so fully investigated by Faraday.

Within this same period we are also to note the remarkable discovery of Diamagnetism by that great man and his researches therein, and the discovery by Seebeck of a whole new class of phenomena under the title of Thermo-electricity, and also the device of those curious and instructive instruments for the production of induced electricity, the Ruhmkorff and Ritchie coils, the Holtz and Toepler and other non-friction electrical machines with their brilliant companions for illustration, the vacuum tubes of Gassiot, Geissler, and Gaiffe, and the cascade of Gassiot; and under the same head we are to make record of the practical applications of these agencies as seen in the blasting of rocks, and the exploding of mines and torpedoes in marine warfare.

We turn next to the field of astronomy, and here it is curious to note, in passing, that a period of fifty years (as referred to by Sir David Brewster) seems to have been the interval between each important step in connection with the great instrument of research in that science—the *Telescope.*

After the telescope of Galileo, came that of Newton; and fifty years after that of Newton, was constructed that of Hadley; fifty years after Hadley's, the instrument of Sir William Herschel, by which so many grand and startling discoveries were achieved.

Fifty years later brings us to our own epoch, when we are permitted to gaze with astonished vision through those marvellous productions of Lord Ross, Alvan Clark, and Lassel; instruments capable of bringing the moon, lying in space 240,000 miles away,(13) to the near distance of 90 miles, revealing its rocks, mountains, valleys, and extinct volcanoes: "the crescent of the planet Venus with its mountainous outline," the system of double and treble stars, the nebulæ, and starry clusters of every variety of shape, and those " spiral nebular formations," which, while they awaken unbounded curiosity and restless speculation, continue to baffle human comprehension. In this domain of science we are called upon to record, as made within the period of which we are now speaking, observations and discoveries of the highest interest. Thus, those regularly recurring showers of meteors, which, within the last half century, have so much attracted the attention of astronomers, and which were first distinctly proved by our countryman, Olmsted, to be rings or groups of bodies, revolving around the sun, in orbits intersecting the pathway of the earth, have, of late, been considered as arranging themselves into some relationship with Cometary forms, and are regarded as being most probably so many great companies of far out-lying skirmishers to those attenuated bodies.

Within this period the list of Asteroids, which was before only *four*, has been increased to more than *one hundred and thirty;* and through the patient toil, philosophical acumen in dealing with the intricate question of planetary perturbations, and the profound mathematical calculations of Leverrier, Adams, and Peirce, a new world has been discovered, to take its place among the sisterhood of planets, having *eight* times the diameter, or more than *five hundred* times the cubical mass of the planet upon which we dwell—a discovery which will shine forth in eternal commemoration of one of the grandest efforts of the human intellect in modern times.

Cognate with astronomy is the science of optics. During the past fifty years whole regions of hitherto unexplored territory have been mapped out;

distinct and totally new branches of the subject have sprung into existence. Indeed, it may be questioned whether any department of human knowledge has been so prolific in discovery and so rich in the accessions of truth within this period as this one of *Light*.

The Emission theory of Newton was opposed, and the doctrine of Wave motion was advocated by Huygen and Euler long anterior, yet the wave doctrine did not take its final shape until a much later period.

The philosophical mind of Dr. Thomas Young, who died no earlier than 1829, had grasped this theory of light, and had contributed much towards establishing it by his experiments and calculations. There was needed, however, some further testimony in its behalf to secure its general adoption. This was supplied by the experiments and mathematical calculations of Fresnell; and it has now become the universally accepted view.

This point established—and it *has* been done within the past five decades—the lifetime to-day of the Franklin Institute, we may now call up, in rapid narration, not attempting any strictly chronological order, some of the more prominent discoveries in this branch of science.

Although Malus had discovered the polarization of light by reflection as early as 1810, and the same philosopher, and Biot and Brewster had a little later, and independently of each other, discovered the same result by refraction, yet we can claim justly for the period in which we are now interested, the addition of many important observations and discoveries which have contributed to render this branch of knowledge one of the most interesting as well as one of the most perfect of the physical sciences. Among the illustrious names to be mentioned in this connection, besides those referred to, are Arago and Sir John Herschel.

While the great improvements referred to, in the telescope, were in progress, the instrument by which we are enabled to look into the intimate structure of the materials around us, was receiving steadily new accessions, both to its power and to the variety of its applications. Although the Microscope, in its early and simple form, was a means of important discovery especially in the structure of organic forms, it was not until within the last fifty years, that it received those improvements, which fitted it for accurate and precise research.

These improvements, commencing with Pritchard, Oberhauser, and Chevallier, and advancing in the workshops of Ross, Powel and Leland, Smith and Beck, Nachet, and others in Europe, and in those of Spencer, Wales, Towles, and Zentmayer in this country, have at length given to the naturalist and Investigator in Physics a means of exploration, which, in the marvels of its discoveries among the almost infinitely small parts of bodies, rivals and perhaps excels the stupendous revelations of the telescope among the masses and spaces of the heavens.

By the increased power and perfection of its composite objectives, and the use of polarizing and other appendages, it has become one of the most precious of our "instruments of precision," giving us, among other results, so clear and faithful a view of the minutest living structure, as to enable us to mark the elementary cell in each stage of its development, and leading us to that great physiological law which makes the living microscopic cell the physical origin of every organic form and of all organic growth.

Nor let us omit to mention, that while thus enlarging our philosophical conception of the relation of living tissues and forms, it becomes in the hands of the physician, an instrument of essential daily use in judging of the nature and seat of disease, guiding to a wise diagnosis and an enlightened treatment.

In connection with the chemical action of light, a vast field of observation and discovery has been explored.

It is probable that *Watt* and *Bolton* in 1799 succeeded in taking *sun pictures* on paper, although no written account of their method has been transmitted to us; and it is well established that in 1802, Sir Humphry Davy and Thomas Wedgewood actually accomplished the same result; but it was not until Niepce and Daguerre, of Paris, between the years 1827 and 1839 successfully devised the method of producing those extraordinary heliographic pictures, known as the Daguerrotype.

Who that is of sufficient age does not remember the amazement and delight with which he first inspected those charming pictures of trees and buildings, landscapes and grazing herds, with all their minutest details sketched by the *sun*, on the silver plate with his own actinic pencil; and then a little later their intense enjoyment through the sentiment involved, of those speaking portraits of loving friends, first produced by our philosophic investigator Prof. Draper?

In 1839 Mr. Fox Talbot first successfully produced
what he called "photogenic" drawings, upon paper
first charged with iodide of silver, then dipped in
nitrate of silver and subsequently in iodide of potassium, and after exposure to the object *developed* to
view, by washing in a mixture of aceto-nitrate and
gallic acid, and finally fixed by means of hyposul-
phite of sodium.

From this has sprung the exquisite art of *modern
photography*, which in its many sided applications
has become a familiar and almost necessary member
of every household.

Quickly following the Talbotype, we have had devised in rapid succession an almost endless variety of
modifications of the paper photograph, and we now
witness as but of yesterday that triumph of patient
skill in this same progress, the Woodburytype, which
first calls upon the sun to paint his faithful picture
upon the sensitized film, then transfers it with un-
failing accuracy to a metallic plate, from which it
may be printed on paper by means of appropriate
ink, as in lithographic or copperplate work.

To this may be added the still more recent, and
perhaps more perfect invention just coming into use,
which, under the name of the Heliotype accomplishes
the same end by printing directly from the film itself,
hardened after it has received the picture.

Nor should we, in this enumeration of the achievements of photography, omit to mention its uses to the
astronomer.

The world has already become familiar with those
remarkable photographic pictures of the moon, obtained by our ingenious countryman, Mr. Rutherford,
in which is depicted, with marvellous fidelity, every

feature of our satellite which the telescope reveals. And at this very moment, another of our country-men, the astronomer Gould, in his observatory at Cordoba, on the plains of the Upper La Plata, is engaged in mapping, by photographic instruments and processes, and with a precision unequalled by any other method, the constellations of the Southern hemisphere.

In 1802, Dr. Wollaston, allowing the light of the sun, after passing through a narrow slit in a darkened room, to fall upon a prism of glass, observed a few dark lines crossing at different places, the prismatic spectrum.

In 1814, the skilful optician, Fraunhofer, counted and mapped as many as 576 of these lines. He ascertained that light so treated, if it were of the *sun*, whether as his direct rays or by reflection, as from the moon or any of the planets, gave these lines always in precisely the same relative position to each other, and to the colors of the spectrum; and, on the other hand, that when the light of the *stars*, which are self-luminous, was so observed, it gave for *each star* its own dark lines, and *differently* located from those of the sun. He was able to assign no reason for these phenomena, but concluded that they were due to a cause *beyond the influence of our Atmosphere*.

After an interval of some years, in which little of direct observation had been made, a new impulse was given to the investigation of these phenomena. J. W. Draper, of this country, M. Faucoult of France, Drs. Balfour Stewart, and Miller of Eng-land, had enunciated a doctrine known as that of "exchanges," more especially in connection with the phenomena of radiation and absorption of caloric.(14)*

This, followed out with the aid of sagacious generalizations and ingeniously devised experiments, in the hands of *Kirchoff*, culminated in that grand discovery which, under the name of *spectrum analysis*, not only furnishes the means of the most delicate qualitative determination of substances even to the discovery of new elements, but extending its powers beyond the earth, has supplied us with a *solar and stellar chemistry*.

Truly the revelations of science are more strange than fiction.

Who that saw with Wollaston, for the first time, a few dark lines traced at intervals across the column of the prismatic spectrum, could have conceived that they should lead to the amazing discoveries and generalizations which have followed, and that to-day we should witness Kirchoff, Bunsen, Huggens, Lockyer, Jansen, and Secchi, pointing their *spectroscope* to the skies to bid the sun, and planets, and stars, and even the comets and nebulæ themselves to reveal to man the hidden secrets of their nature and composition ?

Next in sequence we may properly speak of the kindred branch of science—Acoustics—that fascinating subject which has ever been a source of delight to the student of the laws which govern the pheno-

---

* Dr. John W. Draper has, in the number of "Nature" for July 30th of the present year, entered a reclaimer, in connection with the announcement of the fundamental facts, on which rests the doctrine of Spectrum Analysis. I deem it due that distinguished investigator to quote his statement. See *Appendix*.

mena of sound, and of exquisite enjoyment in its musical relation to the mass of mankind.

Yet it is interesting and singular to note that, while men have lived in the grand musical triumphs of each period in succession, musical composition and execution have been, in a great measure, independent of the science of its physical phenomena. It is, indeed, to be doubted whether Handel, Hayden, Mozart, or Bethoven ever concerned themselves at all with the wave length of this note or that, or whether they even knew accurately the relative length of strings or pipes, which produced one octave above another.

Therefore, since the esthetic relations, and all the charms of music could be realized without the labors of the experimenter and the natural philosopher, it is not unnatural that within the term of years in which we are now particularly interested, no great number of marked discoveries of facts should have been made. Yet so attractive is the whole subject of sound, not only as a study within itself, but in its relations to the phenomena of light and heat, which it is so well adapted to elucidate, it was to be expected that it would be made the theme of extensive *illustration*. Therefore in the department of experimental acoustics, few branches of science have within these recent years witnessed a progress so great. To the ingenuity and skill of Savart, Seebeck, Cladni, Wheatstone, Lissajeau, Helmholtz, Kœnig, Kundt, and Mayer, of Hoboken, we are indebted for the large portion of the instructive apparatus seen at the present time on the counter of the lecture room.(15)

Let us next visit the laboratory of the chemist,

look into the furnace of the metallurgist, and enter the dye-house of the manufacturer, to take account of a few of the results which have been accomplished in these directions within the last fifty years; and here a processson of almost endless length passes before our view.

We witness, just on the verge of the period we are discussing, the first distinct isolation, from Peruvian bark, of that precious alkaloid *Quinia*, whose wondrous sanative powers have rescued so many sufferers from malarious poisoning. We see improvements made in the extraction of nearly all the remedial proximate principles, as Morphia, Quinia, Strychnia, and the like, and the application to purposes of blasting and mining of explosive compounds, Fulminating mercury, Fulminating silver, White Powder, Gun Cotton, and Nitro-glycerine, with its modifications Dinamite and "Giant Powder."

We note the new treatment by Tilghman of fats and oils for the separation of stearic and margaric acid from glycerine for candles, and the uses of that latter substance in medicine as well as in the arts; the manipulation of *Gum-elastic* by which it is on the one hand rendered soluble and suitable to form belting, tubing, bags, and waterproof shoes, coats, blankets, tents, etc., and on the other turned into *Vulcanite* and *Ebonite* with their numberless applications; and of Gutta Percha too, that wonderful gum, so plastic when warm, so firm and resisting when cold, and so highly endowed with electro-insulating power.

We should do injustice to the profound science, and the skill displayed in the chemical arts, did we not here note those magnificent pigments and dyeing materials which have, within recent years, been revealed by the treatment of coal tar, the waste product of gas making. I allude to the various *Aniline colors* whose rich brilliancy of tints vie with the hues of the solar spectrum.

These are all dependent for their production upon the discovery of *Benzole*, made by Faraday.

Among these products we have a black, blue, green, brown, purple, pink, violet, yellow, and a red, adapted for dyeing, for calico printing, the manufacture of the lake pigments and lithographic inks. And, more singular than all, *Alizarine*, which represents the coloring principles of *madder* furnishing the *first* example of the *synthetical* production of a *natural coloring matter*.

Thus we see, derived from the most humble origin, a rich variety of shades wherewith art may adorn her work, or beauty and fashion array themselves.

In immediate connection with this theme, I would here refer to those startling discoveries of Berthelot and others recently given to the world, in which it was ascertained that by the *synthetic* method, or by what may be termed the *inverted process* of chemical reaction, a large number of organic substances may be produced, such as alcohol, wood spirit, grape sugar, formic acid, and vinegar, without the instrumentality of a previous organic substance.

While thus referring to the recent labors of chemistry in works conducing to the power and wealth and civilization of the world, we must not forget those beneficient discoveries which have secured to man immunity from pain in circumstances of otherwise agonizing suffering; for it is to this science that we are indebted for those anæsthetic agents—nitrous oxide gas, ether, and chloroform—which are now so universally employed in medicine and surgery, and which are recognized by all as a precious boon to the operating surgeon, and a priceless blessing to suffering humanity.

Leaving untouched, for want of time, the whole of the sciences of geology and natural history, we may glance at a few of the developments which have been made within the last half century pertaining to mining interests.

At the beginning of this period bituminous coals were taken from the earth in Great Britain and on the continent in quantities measured annually by the few hundreds of thousands of tons; *now*, the quantity is summed up by *millions*. To-day the yearly product of Great Britain alone is not less than *one hundred and ten millions of tons*, an amount, if estimated in mechanical energy, equal to a laboring population of not fewer than *twenty-five millions* of able-bodied men.

We have to record as discovered within this period, the vast beds of anthracite coal, the black diamond of our own State—more precious than the mines of Golconda—which has added so vastly to the prosperity and wealth, not only of this Commonwealth, but to that of the whole country; to refer to the petroleum of our western counties, which, until within recent years, had been known only in small quantity and as a useless object of curiosity, now flowing or being pumped from innumerable artesian wells, and yielding, under chemical treatment, lubricating and burning oils, volatile products, as gasoline, rigolene, etc., with solid paraffine for candles and telegraphic insulating purposes; also to the mines of California, Colorado,

Nevada, Utah, and Australia, rich in their precious treasures of gold, silver, and mercury; and in this connection, to those extraordinary devices of engineering skill, those mountain canals or flumes, and powerful hydraulic jets, for battering down the vast auriferous gravel hills of some of these regions, for the washing out and collection of their precious contents.

In *metallurgic* processes great progress has been made in the extraction and treatment of iron, copper, lead, quicksilver, nickel, aluminium, and the precious metals.

Thus the anthracite furnace has taken the place of the charcoal furnace, and the hot blast has superseded the cold blast in the smelting of iron; and more striking than these is the improved manufacture of steel by the remarkable method of Bessemer, accomplished by driving a blast of air through molten iron just after it has been received from the furnace in a clay-lined crucible, a process which seems destined to revolutionize this great branch of industry.

And still more recently we have to hail as of today, the discovery of that remarkable alloy of copper and tin associated with a small percentage of phosphorus, which seems to endow it with properties of great value. This substance has been named Phosphor-bronze.

In the art of war, too, we are called upon to chronicle vast changes. Whether these changes, which are pointed to as improvements, and as marking a higher civilization, are really blessings or otherwise, depends upon the result, whether a greater and more inevitable destruction of life and property has had the effect of leading more generally to the substitution of arbitration for a resort to arms.

The percussion cap and wafer, with their many modes of use, among them the needle-gun, have superseded the old flint lock; the twisted barrel has replaced the smooth bore ; the turreted monitor has found its way into naval architecture in place of the high-floating ship ; the iron armor has been substituted for the wooden sides, and the light ball has yielded its place to the ponderous steel-pointed missile, charged with its destructive fulminate, until the grim *sarcasm* comes to have a peculiar point, *that ships are made so strong that no balls can pierce them, and balls so heavy, and sent so swiftly that no ships can resist them.*

In the earlier views in regard to the actions and changes of matter, the opinion was entertained that substances were often annihilated, and that with *this* ended all that pertained to them. Thus, that in the burning of a mass of coal, by the combustion it was destroyed, and that the transient heat which it evolved after communicating itself to surrounding objects was then dissipated and lost.

Another view has now come to be adopted, this is, that seeming destruction of a body is only its transformation into some other shape, and the disappearance of the energy attending that transmutation is only the *conversion of one force into another.* The latter statement is, in brief, an expression of the modern doctrine of the " correlation and conservation of the physical forces."

The first step towards this great generalization is doubtless due to our own countryman, Benjamin

Thompson, afterwards Count Rumford, whose famous experiment of the rotation of a solid plunger revolving within a hollow cylinder of iron surrounded by water, demonstrated that heat might be produced for an indefinite length of time by continuous friction, and led him to the sagacious conclusion that the *motion was actually converted into heat;* in other words, that the *visible motion* of the revolving *mass* was changed by the friction into a *vibratory motion* of the *particles* of the apparatus and surrounding water, and that this latter motion constituted the heat developed, that is, that heat is but a "*mode* of *motion*."

This conclusion, in recent years confirmed by various researches and by like processes of experiment and mathematical analysis, through the labors of Mayer, Joule, Grove, Wm. Thompson, Helmholtz, Clausius, Faraday, and Tyndall, has been developed into a comprehensive law now universally accepted, a law which embraces not only mechanical power and heat, but also light, electricity, magnetism, and chemical action in *one grand bond of mutual correlation* or *equivalency*.

To complete the list of topics that might come within the province of the duty assigned me, it would be necessary to transfer to my pages the contents of the scientific and practical journals of the world. I will, therefore, close the enumeration by naming, without adhering to chronological order, only a few out of the many that have a claim to consideration. Thus, the mechanical mowers and reapers, the Ericsson air-engine, the gas-engines of Lenoir and Hugon, the infinite variety of sewing machines, the fog-horn, street railways, the ice ma-

chine, the sand blast of the Tilghman Brothers, the
gunpowder pile-driver, the manufacture of carbonate
of sodium by Le Blanc's process, and the revival of an
old process by the reaction between carbonate of am-
monium and chloride of sodium, the manufacture of
lucifer matches, the preservation of meats and vege-
tables, the silvering of glass by metallic silver instead
of by mercury, the introduction of carbolic acid and
the permanganate of potassium as disinfectants, the
preparation of oxygen by the continuous method,
and of chlorine by the revival of the binoxide of
manganese. And in connection with education, the
creation of institutions for instruction in applied
sciences, of *Institutes of Technology* (16). And, lastly,
in the noble field of benevolence, the introduction
of the humane and merciful treatment of those deprived of reason, in place of the cruelties of the
strait jacket and the terrors of the ducking stool.

Did time permit, I would attempt to recall to
your minds in detail, however imperfect the effort,
wherein this Institute has done its part, but
to do this I should weary your patience. I will,
therefore, simply refer to the experiments it has
conducted in the investigation of the strength of
materials; to its careful search into the causes of
steam-boiler explosions; to the numerous reports of
its committees upon matters within its province; to
its library of valuable scientific and practical works
for consultation; its collections of minerals and
models, the one a help and to give incentive to the
study of an important practical branch of natural
science bearing upon mining interests, the other
facilitating inventive talent; to the courses of instructive lectures delivered during each winter

upon physics, chemistry, geology, and other scientific and practical branches; to its monthly meetings for the reading and discussion of papers upon science and the arts, and the exhibition of novel inventions; and then to those unseen but deeply felt influences which it has exerted, in aiding seekers after information in various directions of thought, by guiding them to persons and authors best capable of supplying their wants.

I would refer also to its Drawing School, where large numbers of young men and women nightly resort, for the acquirement, under able instructors, of that art so valuable in almost every walk of life.

And, lastly, to its Journal, the *pioneer* reporter of the mechanic arts in this country, which, keeping pace with the progress of science and industry, is to-day a living representative of many of the largest interests of our country. With such a record of the past, may not our Institute anticipate yet brighter prospects in the future, and should we not all exclaim in earnest words, " *Esto perpetua*"?

APPENDIX.

(1) In 1763 James Watt, of Greenock, Scotland, devised his first form of *low pressure* Steam Engine. In this engine the steam was condensed directly within the steam cylinder.

In 1765 he introduced the use of a separate condenser, thereby greatly economizing the steam. In this form it was single acting—that is, it received the steam on but one side of the piston, and was only adapted to the purposes of pumping.

In 1784 he caused the steam to act upon both sides of the piston, and thus invented the double-acting engine.

Between this date and 1800 he added many important details—improved the system of condensation, and finally added the cut-off by which the steam could be used expansively, thus perfecting the machine which, in its *great principles* has not since been displaced.

(2) Long anterior to this period Oliver Evans, of Philadelphia, employed a single large tube or flue passing through his boilers, to enable the heated products of combustion to act more efficiently on the water.

It is due to this highly gifted inventor to state that he was the first to put into practical application the use of high steam, in what is now known as the *high-pressure steam-engine* — and that he is also a competitor for the honor of having first applied the paddle wheel to the propulsion of boats.

Prof. Tresca, of the Conservatoire des Arts et Metiers, Paris, in his Treatise on the Steam Engine, awards to Joel Barlow, author of the "Columbiad," the credit of priority in the invention of the *Multitubular* Boiler.

A gentleman who has had access to the original papers of Oliver Evans, has furnished the following statement, which I deem it proper to here quote :—

"The first essential to the modern locomotive, is the high pressure steam-engine, and British writers generally accord it to Messrs. Trevithick and Vivian, who in 1802, took out in England a patent therefor; but, in the American edition of the 2d English edition of Wood's 'Treatise on Railroads,' 1831, Messrs. Trevithick and Vivian are distinctly charged with having copied, without acknowledgment, the plans and specifications of Oliver Evans, which in 1794–5 were sent by him to England, in charge of Mr. Joseph Stacy Sampson. I also find that in a work entitled the 'Young Steam Engineer's Guide,' written by Oliver Evans, and published in Philadelphia in 1805, Mr. Evans speaks of having in 1794–5, sent 'drawings, specifications, and explanations' of his plans to England, 'to be shown to steam engineers.' Mr. Evans also speaks of Mr. Joseph Stacy Sampson, of Boston, who, he states, carried the papers to England, and ' died there, but the papers may have survived.'

"The multitubular boiler, which, next to the high-pressure engine, forms the most essential part of the steam carriage, is by Smiles, who wrote in 1857, accorded to George Stephenson, but I find that both Nicholas Wood, and Dr. Lardner (high British authorties on the steam-engine), who respectively wrote in 1831 and 1835, distinctly declare the multitubular boiler to be due to Mr. Booth, Treasurer of the Liverpool and Manchester Railway, who they state suggested to Mr. Stephenson the use of the tubes, to conduct the heated air through the boiler of his engine—the ' Rocket'—which won the prize in the competitive test on the

Liverpool and Manchester Railway. Indeed, both Mr. Wood and Dr. Lardner concur in stating, that a portion of the £500 prize won by the 'Rocket' was paid to Mr. Booth.

"It is a curious fact that the multitubular boiler in all its essential particulars existed in America almost one-third of a century before its introduction into Great Britain. The boiler which Oliver Evans had devised to generate steam for his high-pressure engine had a tube to conduct the heated air through the water, and in 1803 John Stevens, of Hoboken, New Jersey, took out a patent for a boiler composed entirely of tubes, which, in 1805, he also patented in England. A boiler constructed by Mr. Stevens was '2 feet long, 15 inches wide, and 10 or 12 inches high, and consisted of 81 tubes, 2 feet long, and 1 inch in diameter.' But, unfortunately, all of these tubes were filled with heated water instead of heated air.

"In 1791, Col. James Rumsey, of Virginia, took out a patent for a boiler consisting of 'homogeneous incurvated tubes.' Plans and specifications of all three of these boilers found their way to England; Col. Rumsey's as early as 1792–3. Is it too much to surmise, that the principles of construction they severally developed, ultimately suggested the multitubular boiler of the existing locomotive?

"Smiles claims for Stephenson the introduction of the exhaust steam in the chimney stack, for the purpose of increasing the draught of the furnace, but Nicholas Wood writes that in 'the introduction of those engines it was necessary to resort to the application of waste steam thrown upwards to create a sufficient current of air through the fire.' It seems that to Mr. Hackworth, rather than to Mr. Stephenson, we are indebted for the complete development of the principle.

"Smiles claims for Stephenson the discovery that sufficient adhesion existed between the wheels of the steam carriage and the rails for the purpose of locomotion, but Nicholas Wood, who was present when Stephenson's engine was tried, accords the credit to Mr. Blackett, and, speaking of Mr. Stephenson's engine, writes, 'grooved sheaves were fixed upon the hinder travelling wheels of the engine, and similar grooved sheaves upon the fore wheels of the convoy carriage containing the coals and water, with an endless chain, working over each, to procure the adhesion of the wheels of the convoy carriage, in addition to the adhesion of the engine wheels; but on trial it was not found necessary to resort to the aid of this contrivance.'

" In short, if Nicholas Wood, Dr. Lardner, and others who wrote nearly one-fourth of a century before Smiles, made truthful record, the locomotive owes but little to the inventive genius of Mr. Stephenson. Grave doubts exist as to the validity of every important claim advanced by Smiles for him as the author, or even improver of the steam carriage. Mr. Stephenson doubtless acted an important part in executing the inventions of other and more ingenious minds. But that, and that alone, appears to have been the full extent of the services he rendered.

" But to return to Oliver Evans, of whom the Mechanic's Magazine, published in London in 1850, speaks as the 'first projector of steam travelling.' It appears from the preface to the American edition of Wood on Railroads, that before the termination of the 18th century, Mr. Evans 'urged the adoption of railways and locomotives in lieu of canals.' The same authority declares, that ' Mr. Evans urged in repeated addresses to the public, the construction of a railroad from Philadelphia to New York, and in 1809 attempted to form a company for the purpose of effecting it, purposing the investment of his whole fortune in the enterprise.'

" In order to accomplish his purpose, Oliver Evans—ruthlessly, as it were—stripped from the steam-engine the condenser and air pumps, inventions of the celebrated James Watt, which by him and the world were thought to be absolutely essential thereto. Mr. Evans retained the valve movement due Mr. Watt, with the exception that he introduced the cut-off, and 'thus (to use his own words) the piston is driven by strong puffs of steam, the same that the air-gun drives its bullets.'

" He declared his improvement to be so great ' as to be without a parallel,' but the opponents of innovation were a formidable obstacle to its introduction. Mr. Evans writes that ' those learned in error on this subject oppose their theories, corollaries and demonstrations; those who are well versed in the principles of Watt and Bolton's engine, oppose their darling vacuums. The English steam engineers bring forward their cocks, induction pipes, air pumps, hot wells, sniffling valves, etc. etc.' At length Mr. John Harrison, Messrs. Richards & Simmons, and Messrs. Burtis, Moore & Keen, all of Philadelphia, purchased his engines, and they worked so satisfactorily, that each of the parties indicated concurred in publicly declaring over their respective signatures, 'that they would rather pay Oliver Evans the price of one of his engines, than accept as a present one of English construction.' Edward Mason, Jr., Daniel Bates, Hercules Whitney,

Henry C. Coffin, and Isaac Stanford, all of Providence, Rhode Island, who were mutually concerned in works which they stated required 'great power,' did also over their signatures declare that they had two of Oliver Evans's engines at work, that they had compared it with Bolton and Watt's, 'and after satisfactory investigation we gave Mr. Evans's the preference, and have had it a sufficient time at work to prove its real worth, durability, and cheapness compared with others.' They added that 'his method of warming apartments by the heat of the steam of the engine we consider a new and valuable discovery, consequently the expense of fuel chargeable to the engine is proportionably reduced.'

"From that time forward the use of Mr. Evans's engine became general, and to-day it has so completely superseded that of Mr. Watt, that with the exception of some engine for a steamboat on the rivers running into the Atlantic, the low-pressure engine is almost unknown in the United States.

"In the absence of railways in the United States, Mr. Evans proposed to introduce the steam carriage on turnpike roads, and to that end made a proposition to the President and Directors of the Lancaster Turnpike Company. The original draft of the proposition is on my table as I write. It is dated September 26th, 1804. With his proposition, he directed attention to his inventions and improvements for the manufacture of flour, also to his inventions for making wire cards by machinery, etc. etc. He said, 'This statement I make to you, to show, that I have always hitherto been successful in my mechanical improvements, and have never once failed in any attempt.' But he did fail to induce the company to coöperate. The elevator, that to-day is so much used for the handling of grain, was one of his inventions. Some years before his death, Oliver Evans offered to build a steam carriage that, on a level railway, should run fifteen miles an hour, for double price, if it attained that speed, and nothing if it did not. At the date of this offer (and for many years afterwards) the highest speed of the best English engines was but seven miles per hour. But to his family, and to his intimates, he spoke of a much higher rate of speed. A gentleman has informed the writer, that when he was a youth, Mr. Evans declared to Judge Peters, and other gentlemen present, 'this boy, (putting his hand on the boy's head) 'will live to ride behind one of my engines as fast as a bird can fly,' 'which prediction,' my informant said, 'I have lived to see verified.' It is due to British writers to state, that some of them have gone beyond the patent of Trevithick and Vivian, and have frankly conceded the high pressure engine to Oliver Evans.

"I have thrown the foregoing facts together ; perhaps at some future day a more detailed narrative will show the enormous material benefits that this country—and indeed the entire civilized world—owes to the inventive genius, and unrequited labors of Oliver Evans."

But Mr. Evans never lived to see his darling project of steam travelling by rail fulfilled in the United States.

He died in 1819.

(3) Mr. Joseph Harrison, Jr., of Philadelphia, of the firm of Eastwick & Harrison, in 1839, at the instance of Moncure Robinson, Esq., Civil Engineer of the Reading R. R. Company, designed a new locomotive, intended to have great power for the heavy freighting purposes of that company. This engine was called the "Gowan and Marx." It weighed eleven tons, which was heavy for that day, but light as compared with those of the present.

By the method of disposing of the weight upon the "drivers," it *drew one hundred and one loaded* cars. This was a most valuable step towards the settlement of the problem of cheap transportation of heavy freights on railroads.

(4) M. Moncure Robinson a fait construire pour le chemin de fer de Philadelphie à Pottsville par Reading, qui est destiné à transporter beaucoup de charbon, des locomotives non-seulement à six roues, mais à huit partagées de même en deux trains, et d'une force très-grande. On estime que leur puissance de traction ira à 400 tonnes avec une faible vitesse.

Une de ces machines, le *Gowan et Marx*, a pour diamètre des cylindres 0ᵐ.322 ; la course du piston est de 0ᵐ.406. C'est la plus lourde des machines de la compagnie, et celle dont les cylindres ont le plus grand diamètre. Cependant, *à vide*, elle ne pèse que 9812 kilog., et en marche que 11,100 kilog. Elle es bien loin, comme on voit, de celles qu'on emploie aujourd'hui sur les chemins de fer de l'Europe. Ainsi la compagnie de Saint-Germain à Paris a des machines à détente dont le poids *à vide* es de 16,500 kilog., et où les cylindres ont un diamètre de 0ᵐ.38. Avec de fortes machines comme celles-ci, on obtiendrait sur le chemin de fer de Philadelphie à Mount Carbon des résultats plus satisfaisants encore que ceux qui vont être indiqués.

(5) "On one of its trips (February 20th, 1840), it drew a train of *one hundred and one* four-wheel loaded cars from Reading to Philadelphia, at an average speed of 9.82+ miles per hour, nine miles of the road being a continuous level. The gross load on this occasion was 423 tons, not including the engine and tender, which, if the weight of the tender is counted, equalled *forty times* the weight of the engine."

See "Journal of Franklin Institute," 1840, vol. 25, page 99, Report of G. N. Nichols, Supt. Philadelphia and Reading Railroad, which closes as follows: "The above performance of an eleven ton engine is believed to excel any on record in this or any other country. It may be doubted whether it has been excelled since.

"How strangely this feat of the Gowan and Marx compares with the trials on the Liverpool and Manchester Railroad in October, 1829, but ten years before, when all that was required of the competing locomotives was, that they should draw about *three times* their own weight, tender included, on a level track, five miles long, especially prepared for the trial. The great success of the Gowan and Marx, induced the Philadelphia and Reading Railroad Company to duplicate the plan of this engine in ten engines subsequently built at Lowell, Mass.

"In 1840, the Gowan and Marx attracted the particular attention of the Russian engineers, Colonels Melnikoff and Krafft, who had been commissioned by the Emperor Nicholas to examine into and report upon the various systems of railroads and railroad machinery then in operation in this country and in Europe.

"The result of their examination was favorable to the American system, and when the engineers above named made their report on the construction of a railroad from St. Petersburg to Moscow, an engine upon the plan of the Gowan and Marx was recommended as best adapted to the purposes of this first great line of railroad in the Empire of Russia, and Eastwick and Harrison were requested to visit St. Petersburg with the view of making a contract for building the locomotives and other machinery for the road.

. "Mr. Harrison went to St. Petersburg in the spring of 1843, and in connection with Mr. Thomas Winans, of Baltimore, a contract was concluded with the government of Russia, at the close of the same year, for building 162 locomotives, and iron trucks for 2500 freight cars. Mr. Eastwick joined Mr. Harrison and Mr. Winans at St. Petersburg in 1844."

(6) Although the propeller in its cruder forms had been attempted many years before, no practically successful application of the screw seems to have been made until 1836 and 1837. At which time the result was accomplished by Sir Francis Pettit Smith and Captain John Ericsson respectively, between whose claims of priority there has been a difference of opinion.

"Within the past ten years the screw has entirely replaced the paddle in transatlantic navigation, the weight of marine engines has decreased one-half, the steam pressure has quadrupled, and the consumption of coal has diminished two-thirds." (North American and United States Gazette.)

For further information on this subject the reader is referred to the "Encyclopædia Britannica," Article "Steam Navigation," and Bourne's "History of Screw Propulsion."

(7) The Sirius left London for New York April 4th, 1838, and arrived at New York April 22d, making the clear voyage in seventeen days.

The Great Western left Bristol on April 7th, 1838—three days later—and reached New York on the 23d, making the voyage in fifteen days.

(8) Of these presses the Walter seems to take precedence in rapidity of work and simplicity of construction.

The inventors of the Walter Printing Press claim for it the following points :—

"1st. It is a perfecting machine—printing on both sides at the rate of 12,000 copies per hour, or from 10,000 to 11,000, including stoppages. Ample provision has been made for overcoming the difficulties of set-off; and, as there are only four composition rollers used, and great care has been taken to make the cutting and delivering processes certain, the liability to interruption is reduced to a minimum. When changing from one reel to another, the arrangements are such that the delay scarcely exceeds a minute, and the reels are kept as large as possible for convenient handling.

"2d. The labor employed when the Walter Press is in operation consists of two lads taking off, who suffice to expect and count each sheet, and a striker to start the machine and look after the reels as they are unwound. One overseer can easily superintend two presses; capable of turning out, with six unskilled hands, perfected sheets at the rate of from 20,000 to 22,000

6

per hour, stoppages included. With four of these presses—twelve lads and two overseers—'The Times' is now printed at the rate of more than 40,000 copies per hour; (*i. e.*) in less than half the time and with one-fifth the number of hands required by the fastest and best printing machines previously in use. Moreover, layers-on, who are highly-trained workmen, and must be paid accordingly, are entirely dispensed with.

"3d. Attention is directed to the extreme simplicity of the Walter Press in all its details. There is nothing about it liable, with the usual ordinary care, to get out of order; while a practically unlimited rate of production is secured by the repetition of stereotype plates on additional machines to any extent that may be required. Thus, newspapers of large circulation can be printed with maximum economy of time and labor, and with a freedom from risk in the process of production never before attainable. The waste of paper may be stated at ¼ per cent., but in connection with the change of system newspaper proprietors and printers will at once find that they obtain a knowledge of the kind of article which is supplied by their papermakers—how it counts and weighs per ream, and what degree of uniformity it is produced—never before realized. There is a considerable saving of ink also, and in blankets and rollers. The exclusive use of stereotype plates releases the ordinary type from all wear and tear; so that a fount lasts at least ten times as long as it could under the former system. It is hardly necessary to add that with the Walter Press the register must be practically perfect."

The Walter Press is used by the London Times, London Daily News, Edinburgh Scotsman, also by a paper in Manchester, New York Times, and St. Louis Republican.

(9) "Mr. Wm. Sturgeon, a native of London, about the year 1825, discovered that when wires of soft iron were placed within the coil of a conducting wire, they were rendered intensely magnetic."—*Annals of Philos.*, vol. xii. p. 359.

"Our knowledge of this subject was afterwards greatly extended during the period from 1828 to 1831, by the researches of Professor Henry, Secretary of the Smithsonian Institution, at Washington."

"The instrument first used by Professor Henry, in 1828, to illustrate electro-magnetic action, consisted of an iron bar, two inches square, twenty inches long, bent in a horse-shoe form, and weighing 21 pounds. The keeper weighed 7 pounds, and 540 feet of insulated copper wire were wound in nine coils of 60 feet each around the horse-shoe shaped bar of soft iron. From the experiments which he made with it, he proved that a small battery is capable of producing great magnetic effects, if the spirals of the coil are numerous, and the resistance to the passage of electricity is not very great. He also showed the effect of varying the lengths of the conducting wires and the intensity of the current, and found that six short wires were more powerful than three of double the length. When the current was made to pass through all of the nine coils, the magnet raised seven hundred and fifty pounds.

"Subsequently, Professor Henry constructed two of the largest and most powerful instruments of this kind at present known. One now in the cabinet of Yale College, weighing 59½ pounds, which sustained a weight of 2063 pounds; another, belonging to the cabinet of Princeton College, N. J., of 100 pounds weight, which could support 3500 pounds, or one and a half tons."

(10) Prof. Henry says that, "in 1832, nothing remained to be discovered in order to reduce the proposition of the electro-magnetic telegraph to practice. I had shown that the attraction of an armature could be produced at any distance, and had designed the kind of a battery and coil around the magnet to be used for this purpose. I had also pointed out the fact of the applicabiliiy of my experiments to the electro-magnetic telegraph. I make a distinction between the terms discovery and invention. The first relates to the development of new facts; the second to the application of these or other facts to practical purposes."—*House Case*, p. 93. (See Lectures on Magnetic Telegraph, by Laurence Turnbull, M.D., p. 39.)

(11) The most improved forms of the magneto-electric machines are those of Holmes, of Siemens, of Wild, of Ladd, and of Gramme.

(12) While speaking of the Battery, let us not forget nor ignore the inventions of one of the benefactors of science of our own country, who, a little more than fifty years ago, feeling deeply the want of more *convenient* forms, devised arrangements, which were, at that time, by far the most perfect which had been constructed.

I refer to the Calorimotor, Deflagrator, and Tilting Batteries of Dr. Robert Hare, late Professor of Chemistry in the Medical Department of the University of Pennsylvania, described in 1819.

The various forms of the modern *non-constant* Battery, in which either the plates are lowered into the liquid, or the liquid is lifted to the plates, are in mechanical *principle* but a reproduction of his Calorimotor and Deflagrator, affording but another illustration where science, like history, often repeats itself.

(13) This statement is true at least of Mr. Alvan Clark's great refractor lately erected in the National Observatory, Washington.

RECLAIMER OF DR. DRAPER.

(14) In my memoir "On the production of light by heat" (Phil. Mag., May, 1847), I established experimentally the following facts :—

1. All solid substances and probably liquids become incandescent at the same temperature.

2. The thermometric point at which some substances become red hot is about 977 Fahrenheit degrees.

3. The spectrum of an incandescent solid is continuous ; it contains neither bright nor dark fixed lines.

4. From common temperatures nearly up to 977° F., the rays emitted by a solid are invisible. At that temperature they are red, and the heat of the incandescing body being made continuously to increase, other rays are added, increasing in refrangibility as the temperature rises.

5. Whilst the addition of rays so much the more refrangible as the temperature is higher is taking place, there is an augmentation in the intensity of those already existing.

This memoir was published in both American and European journals. An analysis of it was read in Italian before the Royal Academy of Sciences at Naples, July, 1847, by M. Melloni, which was also translated into French and English.

Thirteen years subsequently M. Kirchhoff published his celebrated memoir "On the relations between the coefficients of emission and absorption of bodies for light and heat." A translation of this memoir may be found in the *Philosophical Magazine*, July, 1860.

In this memoir, under the guise of mathematical deductions, M. Kirchhoff, taking as his starting-point the condition discovered by Angström in 1854, respecting the relations between the emitting and absorbing powers of different bodies for light and heat, among other things deduces the following facts. I give them as they are succinctly stated by M. Jamin in his "Cours de Physique de l'école Polytechnique" (1869).

1. All bodies begin to be red-hot at the same moment in the same space, and become white-hot at the same time.

2. Black bodies begin to emit red rays near 525° C. (977° F.)

3. The spectrum of solids and liquids is devoid of fixed lines.

4. The rays first emitted by black bodies are red; to these are added successively and continually other rays, increasing in refrangibility as the temperature rises.

In his celebrated memoir, and in subsequent publications on the history of spectrum analysis, M. Kirchhoff abstains from drawing attention to the coincidences I am here pointing out, except that in a foot-note to his memoir he makes in a single word allusion to mine. But from this no one would infer what were really the facts of the case, and accordingly in the bibliographical lists subsequently published, in works on spectrum analysis, such as those of Prof. Roscoe and Dr. Schellen, my memoir is not noticed.

I earnestly solicit those who take an interest in the history of spectrum analysis to compare my memoir in the *Philosophical Magazine*, May, 1847, with those published by M. Kirchhoff thirteen years subsequently, on the radiating and absorbing powers of bodies (Phil. Mag., July, 1860), and on the history of spectrum analysis (Phil. Mag., April, 1863).

JOHN WILLIAM DRAPER.

University, New York, July 8.

(15) Among the more recent additions to our knowledge in this branch of science, we may mention, the explanation of the cause of dissonance, and the analysis of quality of tones and a physiological theory of music by Helmholtz; the discovery in the ear of the cords of Corti, by the investigator of that name, the duration of acoustic impressions, and the mapping of sound waves, by Mayer, of the Stevens Institute, Hoboken; the influence of the transverse movement of air upon sound, by Tyndall; and the multitude of instruments for illustrations, constructed, and many of them devised, by Kœnig.

(16) A number of our institutions of learning have within recent years enlarged their scope of instruction, by associating with their classical and literary department, a "Department of Science," in which certain practical branches are taught, and made elective by the student. The more prominent of these are, the "Lawrence Scientific School," of Harvard; the "Sheffield Scientific School," of Yale College; the "School of Mines," of

Columbia College; and the "Scientific Department," of the University of Pennsylvania.

Among the institutions which have been active in advancing the study of applied science in this country, the Massachusetts Institute of Technology would seem to claim especial notice on account of the peculiarities of its organization, and its influence on other scientific schools. Founded in 1861, according to the plans, and under the direction, of Prof. William B. Rogers, it set the example of making laboratory-work a chief means of scientific training even in the early stages of study ; and was the first to take the important step, since so generally followed in this country, of organizing a "*Physical Laboratory*," where the student, after being instructed in the simple manipulations, is gradually trained to the more difficult researches in experimental physics. See "Objects and Plan of an Institute of Technology," 1860, and "Scope and Plan of the Massachusetts Institute of Technology," 1864.

In introducing the third speaker, the President said, that about nine years ago there was an attempt made to remodel the working machinery, as it were, of the Institute, to fit it for a greater usefulness, and certain changes were deemed necessary in the by-laws. It was decided to abolish the offices of Recording and Corresponding Secretaries, and in place thereof to appoint a Resident Secretary, who should be a salaried officer. It was required that he should be a gentleman of literary and scientific attainments. Now there was in our midst a young man, a graduate of our university, who tried to study law, but drifted into science, and who was rapidly making for himself a name as a scientist. He was selected to fill this new office, and right well did he do so; but others saw and recognized his worth. In our neighboring State across the Delaware, there lived for many years a man noted as an engineer; at his death he gave from his great estate abundant means to found a school for the teaching of mechanics. The trustees, having prepared a suitable building, looked about then for some fitting person to act as President, and our very useful secretary soon received a call to take this position of greater usefulness. We cannot but feel proud that under his care this school for mechanics has prospered, and to-day we welcome its President to our midst. Ladies and gentlemen, I introduce as the next speaker, Prof. HENRY MORTON, President of the Stevens Institute of Technology, of Hoboken, N. J.

ADDRESS OF PROF. HENRY MORTON.

LADIES AND GENTLEMEN:

In discussing my theme this evening I propose to begin at the beginning, and set out from the very origin of the subject, and yet, so rapid are our modern modes of thought as to travel that, if we do not run off the track, ten minutes will easily see us safely arrived at the end of the matter.

My first proposition is a brief though comprehensive one. It is simply this. Ladies and gentlemen, The earth moves! And though as I perceive you are not electrified by this important statement, I yet hope within a few minutes to show you that, taken in its full and true significance, this assertion may be as wonder-exciting now, as in its simpler meaning it was two hundred and fifty years ago, when a Galileo only dared to say it in a whisper.

At the present time we have gone far beyond being surprised to hear that the fixed and solid earth is not the stationary centre of the universe, and are not even made giddy when we think that it is spinning at a rate of about 1000 miles an hour (for the equator),and flying around the sun with a velocity of 1000 miles a minute, or about 1000 times faster than an express train behind time. We are not even shocked to learn that, beside these two motions, our earth, as part of the solar system, is on its travels through space in an unknown path at an unknown rate; or as it may be otherwise expressed, is one of the planetary lambs which the sun-shepherd is leading through the celestial fields, browsing as they go on such shooting stars, meteors, or comets as may come within their reach. Familiarity has enabled us to accept as perfectly commonplace and natural, all these ideas of instability and motion, and we now would only be astonished if some one were to say to us that the world *did not* move.

Aggressive science, however, which is itself never willing to rest, but makes each advance only a new base for further progress, will not leave us even here, but points us to an entirely different class of motions and says: Not only does the world and every object in the universe move, but *it is the motion of all matter which gives it those properties by which we recognize it.*

In other words, if the matter of the universe were to be brought to a state of rest, it would no longer be the universe, it would no longer be matter as we can comprehend that idea ; or in yet other words, matter is matter, the universe is the universe as much by reason of the motion of its individual atoms as by reason of their actual existence.

Example is better than precept, and I will therefore take a case and give you two views—the external or artistic, and the interior, or scientific of the same scene.

We are in a valley among snow-capped mountains, and before us a lake spreads its mirror to the sky.

No breath of air ripples its surface, no wavelet breaks upon its beach, nothing is there but absolute repose. So says the artist, and painting such a scene he calls his picture " Silence," " Repose," " The Lake of Dreams," or some such appropriate title.

Now, however, let us look at that same scene with eyes touched by the wand of science, and opened to see beneath the surface of things. What do we then behold? Is there any longer an impression of repose? Of rest? Of sleep?

Look at that mass of water with its mirror-like surface. We see there a perfect Sebastopol of flying missiles, water atoms hurled in clouds from the surface into the air, water atoms hurled back from the air into the water surface. It is by such action as this, science shows us, that evaporation takes place, or the invisible though rapid passage of the liquid water into the viewless air.

The whole mass of the water is likewise thrilling through with those heat motions, of which if deprived partially, it would freeze into ice, and if robbed utterly, would shrink into some formless horror, of which even the imagination of science can form no picture.

We turn now to the breezeless air, and here again we see that it *is* air, and not some densest solid, or nameless nonentity, only because of the ceaseless flight of its countless molecules, which, rebounding, jostling, ricocheting, glancing, but ever on the wing of motion, make it the light, elastic fluid which we know as air.

And if we next turn to the towering rocks and snow-capped peaks, we will find the same conditions in a modified form. All undoubtedly thrill with the quick heat-pulse which is the very soul of matter,

and in probability owe their distinctive character-
istics to peculiar modes of motion among their atoms.
But it is needless to go further in this direction.
It is evident that in the view of science the "universe
of matter" is *as* truly the " universe of motion."
Realizing this fact, is there any evident deduction
to be drawn that bears upon the object which has
brought us together this evening?

Placed as rulers and as student of this universe of
matter in motion, and becoming rulers and masters
of its resources just in proportion as we are apt and
faithful students, what is the branch of study to
which we should most devote our attention? Evi-
dently that which treats of matter in its relations
to motion, and this subject I need hardly say is
known by the name of Mechanics, and is that to the
development of which the Franklin Institute has
directly and indirectly contributed for the last fifty
years.

That you may not suppose I have laid undue stress
upon this point, allow me to quote a few words from
a late enunciation of one of the greatest students of
science, Helmholtz. "If, however (and the previous
context gives these words the force of, As therefore),
motion is the primordial change which lies at the
root of all other changes occurring in the world,
every elementary force is a force of motion, and the
ultimate aim of physical science must be to determine the movements which are the real causes of all
other phenomena, and discover the motive power on
which they depend ; in other words, to merge itself
into mechanics."

We may then fairly say that, in its relations to the
universe at large, and to man's knowledge of those
material surroundings on which his prosperity so

largely depends—the work of the Franklin Institute, founded "for the promotion of science and the mechanic arts," has been a noble one judiciously directed!

We may, however, well ask if there is any reason why at this particular time, at this special epoch in the world's history, such a subject should be more than ever appropriate and desirable?

The comparison of national growth or human progress with the development of a child, is of course familiar, and has been frequently suggested, but is none the less apt and fruitful in valuable indications.

Thus we see in the infant, or in the infancy of the human race, at first only physical growth and development, the strength and muscular powers of the savage and of the barbarous nation.

Then comes in the child the period of growing intelligence, first developed through the perceptions of sense and the workings of the imagination, that period when the literature of the fairy-tale flourishes, and Cinderellas and Bluebeards people the world.

To this we find, as a parallel in the history of the race, the period of mythology, and the "golden age" of the poets.

Next to this in the well-ordered training of the child comes the first idea of moral relations, of duty, of piety, of a divine superior; and to this we find in the world's history the corresponding period of revelation, and the introduction and spread of Christianity.

Then in the child comes the education in methods of expression. The child learns to read, to write, to express himself, and to grasp the thoughts of others in various languages.

To this we find a parallel in the age of reviving

learning, when the great schools of Europe were founded and flourished, and taught the classics, rhetoric, logic, and other cognate subjects, all having a direct bearing upon modes of expression.

Now when the child has mastered these preliminaries, what is his next step, if he does the best for the development of his own powers, and for his usefulness, to the world at large? You will at once answer me, he goes out from the shelter of the scholastic walls into the world of nature, he comes in contact with its facts, the laws of the material universe, and aided by the physical strength, stimulated by the imagination, restrained by the moral sense, guided by the intellectual training which he has received, he begins the real battle of life, and wrests from nature, by his own exertions, that which shall sustain and benefit himself and his species.

What then may we look for from the race which, at this present point in its career, has gone through the same preparation, but that *it* should address itself to the same work, and with frame, heart, soul, and intellect sufficiently trained for the task, turn to the great labor of developing from the inexhaustible stores of the universe, the vast material benefits which there await its research, to awake into beneficent energy?

For ourselves, and with reference to our own action in the future, this comparison, which we have just made, is also suggestive.

This great boy (the human race) we see is in his workshop, and if we want to give what will be of most use and pleasure to the sturdy youth, we must not select new toys, new fairy-tales, new tracts, or new grammars, but new *tools*.

He needs no new games for his amusement, no

new romances to develop his imagination, surely no
new religions to guide his soul, and no new languages to express his thoughts ; but he can make
the best use of any quantity of *new tools*, and of the
opportunity and instruction for their employment.

AT the subsidence of the emphatic applause
offered to Prof. Morton, the President of the Institute, Mr. COLEMAN SELLERS, arose and addressed the
assembly.

ADDRESS OF MR. COLEMAN SELLERS,

PRESIDENT OF THE FRANKLIN INSTITUTE.

IT is well nigh forty years ago, I think, that
Professor James P. Espy, the storm king, as he was
called, taught school in the Franklin Institute building. The present model room was his school-room.
Somehow, ever since the time when that enthusiastic
old gentleman tried to pound learning into me—as
was the wont in those days of birch rod and ratan
rule—the Franklin Institute has been connected in
my mind with instruction, with learning. No more
fitting time perhaps than now, at the close of its
fifty years of usefulness, to tell how it has taught,
how it can teach, and what need there is, in these
days of progress, for certain kinds of instruction not
yet obtainable in our common schools.

It was in the first years of this century that Dr.
Birkbeck, of Glasgow, conceived the idea of lecturing
to artisans on subjects that would aid them in their
callings. His scheme took well ; his lecture-room
was crowded, and able men volunteered to aid him

in his laudable enterprise. During the years 1823 and 1824 the first Mechanics' Institute took shape as the outgrowth of what Dr. Birkbeck had done, and he very properly was called to preside over the first one founded in London. Mr. Brougham, afterwards Lord Brougham, was prominent in its organization. This was being done in England at the very time our Franklin Institute of the State of Pennsylvania for the promotion of the Mechanic Arts was coming into existence. With the foundation of the London Society all England and Scotland seemed to waken to the need of scientific instruction for the mechanics and artisans—and in all the great towns, even in some villages, Mechanics' Institutes sprang up, to lead a short life of active usefulness, then to languish and to die. These Mechanics' Institutes were not organized by mechanics—they were originated by philanthropic persons, who, seeing the need of a higher education of the working classes, spent their time and their money in this direction. They failed, simply because those for whom they were created would not avail themselves of their advantages.

Our Franklin Institute was from the beginning a Mechanics' Institute, in one sense of the word. It taught by lectures, and sometimes by classes, but it was always more than was contemplated by the societies abroad. If I may so express myself, it was, and still is a democratic learned society; it is not exclusive. No well-behaved person is excluded from its membership. All who desire to reap its benefits, or to aid it in its great work of promoting the mechanic arts, can join it. This is not so with the so-called learned societies of this and other lands. They select their members from among those who

have already distinguished themselves in the arts
or sciences, or are likely so to distinguish themselves; hence, their membership is confined solely
to the learned of the land. Now, mark the difference in our case. Learned men join our society, and
in its hall come in contact with those who may be
unlearned, so far as books are concerned, but better
informed in some special art or trade. Theory and
practice are brought together, and each helps the
other. Distinguished scientists admit that they are
indebted to this association for information of a
practical character, probably not readily obtainable
otherwise. While on the other hand we, each one
of us, know how we have been benefited by their
learning, and with what attentive earnestness we
listen to their words.

In the youth of our Institution, when this now
vast city was comprised within narrow limits, when
those who frequented our halls were less scattered
than now, each day and each evening there came
together a little band of congenial spirits—mechanics,
artisans, and professors, who labored earnestly to
carry out the great aim of the society, and who were
at all times willing to sink their personality in the
good of the society. Their work was the work of
the Franklin Institute, not of its individual members. Among those men who gave their best time
and energy to this labor were many men neither
mechanics, artisans, nor professsonal scientists, but
lovers of the arts and sciences. Looking over the
pages of the members' roll—many such names occur
—few, indeed, of the early ones are here to listen to
my words to-night. With one, however, I have
talked much of late, and from him learned very
many interesting facts relating to the Institute. It

was in his office that some of the first meetings were held that led to its organization, and his knowledge of its workings extends through its entire career. We had earnestly hoped that he would have addressed you this evening, but his strength was not equal to the task. So I promised him to say to you it is his firm conviction that the vitality of the Institute is in the union, the close union and mutual reaction of theory and practice. He recounted many incidents to show how meritorious inventors had been aided by disinterested theorists; how timely warning from the better informed in what had been done has saved many a fruitless ramble over already well-trodden ground in the search for novelties. My first recollections of the workings of our society are inseparably connected with his name. He was a member of the first committee upon which I served, and his wonderful memory was my astonishment then as it is now. His mind was an open encyclopædia to us all, and it was from the kind interest taken by him and by others like him in our scientific labors that we received the greatest encouragement in our work. I have ventured to take this kind gentleman, Mr. GEORGE WASHINGTON SMITH—as an example of disinterested labor—because he was neither a mechanic nor a professional scientist, but nominally a lawyer (I know not if he practised law), a scholar by preference, and a lover of all that tends to advance the material welfare of his countrymen. It was the work done by him and many others like him in the active, thankless duties of the scientific committees, that made many of our most valuable reports of so great use to the world at large. Among these hard workers were young men who subscribed their names to the constitution with no calling as yet selected to mark their position in life—many of them since known to fame. In that long roll, too, may be found names of men now noted and honored in the arts, who in the beginning inscribed after their signatures callings and trades little indicative of their after greatness. These men were educated practically in the Franklin Institute; it was there their minds received direction. Thus the Franklin Institute has prospered in its teaching—in its teaching of men by men. Out of the town that saw the beginning of our society fifty years ago, Philadelphia has now spread over an entire county, and in area is, perhaps, the largest city in the world under one municipal government, and to-day it stands in the front ranks of industry. To say it is the Manchester of America is saying but part of the truth. The world in congress at Paris and Vienna recognized this, and gave first honors to our workmen. Philanthropists from abroad visit us and ask to be shown the place where the working people—not crowded in filthy tenement-houses and hovels—live each in his own home—his neat, comfortable home; and they seek to know how far education has progressed among the makers of the wealth of the world. They know full well that the rudiments of science, at least, are needed by all mechanics in all trades; they know full well that the great universal language of mankind, the language of the pencil, the picture language, is the very foundation of all the arts; everything that is to be made, at least well made, must be first drawn, must find its shape on paper. They visit our common schools, and they note that the pupils have plenty of grammar, plenty of geography, and spelling, and reading, and so on, but barely rudiments

7

of science, and scarcely any drawing whatever; this, too, when the world is crying aloud for technical education. How strange it must seem to those who come to us from the old countries, where the schools of art are side by side with the museums and the great art galleries, and where all these great collections are open to their advantage, each and every day of the week, where the use of the pencil, the only universal language of the world, is taught with the a, b, c's of their native tongue. We can indeed say, that for well nigh fifty years, the Franklin Institute has tried to remedy this defect. There almost only can the young mechanic obtain the principles of the art. It is true, our noble Academy of Fine Arts throws open wide its doors to those who can take the time to avail themselves of its classes, and the School of Design for Women, an outgrowth of our Institution, does its part; the High School, with its night classes for artisans, helps in the work; but of the thousands of children who pass each year through our common schools, how few can avail themselves of the chances, how few know the need of the art that underlies all other arts?

Our common school education gives us traders, gives us shopkeepers, but it gives us no artisans. I know not if this can be remedied, but I do know we require some other training for our sons and our daughters.

But two years hence all the nations of the earth will be represented in our park—they will bring with them the work of their hands and their brains. Then will our people be able to see and judge for themselves how early education reacts on art, and how much need we have for cultivation and refinement to exalt the faculties of our artisans. Go into our great industrial establishments, and seek out the modellers and the designers, the draughtsmen, speak to them, and many times you will be greeted with the accents of a foreign tongue. True we pay high wages, and the educated designers of Europe will make their home on our shores. But why not train our children to fill these places? Most unquestionably there is a freshness of thought and an originality of conception in the products of American ingenuity, but they lack, sadly lack in some respects, a cultivated and refined appreciation of the beautiful.

There was a time not fifty years ago when the workshops of Philadelphia competed only one with another. Trade was confined to narrow limits; with little competition there was little need of economy and careful calculation in the conduct of our factories. Now the railroad, the steamship, and thought borne on the wings of lightning, have broken down all geographical barriers, and the workshops of Philadelphia find competitors in the workshops and cheap labor of the oldest lands. How are we to hold the van in this strife but by more excellent productions more cheaply produced? How are we to achieve this result but by putting more brains in our work? Say not to me that learning unfits our men for work. I tell you proper instruction is what our working people most need—what the Franklin Institute has ever tried to give them. There is in the world drudgery to be done, drudgery that needs no brain work, but there will be through all times enough stupidity to satisfy all the wants in this direction, and intelligent laborers will make their heads save their hands to their own profit and the benefit of the whole human family. That a means of educating our young men and young women in the direction

of practical industries is greatly needed is evinced by
the change now progressing in our higher schools.
Over our broad land technical colleges are springing
up, and students are crowding their halls. In our
midst the University of Pennsylvania, coupled with
whose history is the name of Franklin, whose professors and teachers are our own active fellow-mem-
bers, but a little while ago reared for itself vast halls
for learning, yonder on the west bank of the Schuyl-
kill—this, to make room for science, to enable our
young men to fit themselves to be engineers, to be
architects, to be what they will. The learning there
acquired is with an aim. The student has a profession before him, and he prepares himself for his life's
work. These schools and colleges do but a part of
the work; it is with men as men, they must continue
their training.

Fathers and mothers of my dearly loved country,
believe me no want is so deeply felt in this land as
the want of practical, technical education. Give to
your sons and to your daughters a sound foundation
of useful learning; teach them the pleasures, the
dignity of skilful manual labor; make their minds
leaders of their hands, and teach their hands to be
willing servants to their minds. It was but the
other day that a chemist in a rolling mill would
have been laughed at by the practical iron masters
of the land. Now, a leading engineer says on the
public rostrum, that the future of our iron interests
is in the hands of our chemists, in the laboratory,
and in learning. Would you have your children
take part in this great work? Remember that in
all our workshops there are places for but few of
them as learners, as apprentices. Give to them,
therefore, that instruction that will make them of

value in the land, that will cause them to be selected for places of trust; for the contest in the world's industries in the future is to be fought with brains, not with hands alone.

The Franklin Institute has for fifty years been laboring in the direction of the scientific education of mechanics, and proud are its members of the work it has done. Yet how true the words seem, that came to us last Tuesday in our Public Ledger, when it told the story of this Society's usefulness, and said, " its achievements, we believe, have been more thoroughly recognized and appreciated everywhere than here in its own home. This is said to be characteristic of Philadelphia, that it does not ' exploit' its own good works. It would be well if our people were of a different habit in this respect, and it would be better if, at the fiftieth anniversary of the Institute on Tuesday next, at Musical Fund Hall, there should be inaugurated a new era of the recognition and appreciation of its merits, its services, its great usefulness, and its honorable record. If Boston possessed such an institute, with such a history, its renown would not be allowed to become dim at home by any lack of public proclamation of what it is and what it has done."

Citizens of Philadelphia, your Institute's usefulness is limited only by its pecuniary means. Its fifty years' work has been done with but little money to do it with. No liberal endowment has placed it beyond want, and rigid economy has barely eked out the yearly contributions to meet the most pressing wants. Shall it be so in the future? It is not asked that you give to it, hoping for no return. What we want is your good names added to our list of members. In a population of well nigh a million, scarcely

900 names are on our roll of members. All the world abroad knows and honors our Institute. Talented men in distant cities ask to be, and are proud to be, considered members of it. Will not you join us in our task, and when the Centennial of our nation's freedom is being celebrated in our midst, say to your guests that you are members of the Franklin Institute?

Working men of Philadelphia, let me rather say fellow-workmen of America, my most earnest sympathies are with you in all your efforts towards self-improvement. My own path in life started from the school-house through as lowly walks in life as any of yours. If fortune has led me to higher usefulness, believe me it has been not without diligent application and hard study. To you the Franklin Institute opens its doors and affords you a sure way of increasing your store of knowledge. Attend its lectures, be present at its meetings, give from your store of practical experience freely, take in return what others can give to you. It will be to you as it has been to me and to others—a school of great value. Trust me, the teaching of man by man in frequent intercourse is the most potent means of acquiring knowledge, and knowledge well applied is indeed a power.

At the close of Mr. Sellers's address the meeting adjourned.

LINES

ON THE FIFTIETH ANNIVERSARY OF THE FRANKLIN INSTITUTE.

BY AN OLD MEMBER.

OUR golden Pentecostal year has passed,
And the new Fifty whitens in the east.
How few and far between the Fathers stand
Though sought with keenest eye amid the throng !
As memory summons the old roll anew
The chilling silence falls upon our hearts ;
At length with strange deliberate haste they speak
And point us to the bright propitious sky
That glows above and well predicts the triumph.

Those fifty years ! shall we not spare a glance
To mark their mission and the sheaves they bring,
Ere stern Oblivion swings his shadowy door
Which ever hides our best and loved too soon ?—
Those seven-times-seven-and-one may well atone
For the slow slumbering thousands which precede them.

Surely the era is our FRANKLIN'S own ;
And let no other name with his intrude,
As harness'd on the iron gossamer
The *silent* thunder under his strong spell
Yoked with the carrier dove, submissive bears
Our griefs or greetings through the ambient sky,
Or (strange alternative) with equal speed
Invades the horrid depths of ocean's caves,
Stirring their monsters with unwonted thrill
While hurrying by charged with the fate of nations !
The Twins of Fire and Water, whose joint might
Archimedes dare not anticipate,
Attained their manhood's stature in this term,
So emulous to urge the towering barque
Through angriest seas, or drive the rampant car
That on its thousand miles of prairie plain
But gathers breath to climb the mountain side !

We range these startling marvels in the van,
Yet nobler victories are on our scroll,
Which ask no heralding by sound of trumpet,
But, like the morning light, the evening dew,
Fall indiscriminate and silently :—
The myriad Loom that surfeits Fashion's call ;
The tireless Needle even in the race ;
The subtle Essence of the cumbrous Lamp
Spread through dark iron arteries by miles
Yet answering to our beck in every loft,
In cellar, hall, or chamber, day and night ;
The Planting Plough and rolling Reaping Car
Which seem to hail each other in the field
And mix their tasks in wondrous harmony ;
The Anvil shaped and burnished like a shrine ;
The Hammer quiv'ring like the humming-bird ;
Light's mild mysterious picture which presents
Face of Apelles from Apollo's hand ;
Again, the seeming ravage of the Rainbow,
That plucks its tints apart as in the fable
Penelope undid her patient web,
Yet while we gaze begins the retribution —
From the dread depths of space comes laden back
With hidden truths extorted from the stars ;
And last, the Sovereign Press, ordained to hurl
The bolt that surely smites or sanctifies
Art's endless work through the wide realm of mind !

Such are our peaceful triumphs that look down
From the blue arch of half a century,
As constellations o'er the heads of all ;
Whose smile surrounds—pervades our model dwellings,
Where labor shares refinement without pride,
As Philadelphia's peculiar fare !

The iridescent rays of scattered power
Our INSTITUTE collects and concentrates,
Then sends them forth in scientific phalanx
To conquer nature and to bless mankind.
This was the high ambition of its founders
Who (like the steward in the parable)
O'er the few things allowed them have been faithful.
May those who follow have the full "ten talents,"
And well improve the new and larger trust !